LITERARY THEORY

LITERARY THEORY

Jonathan Culler

A BRIEF INSIGHT

STERLING

New York / London
www.sterlingpublishing.com

STERLING and the distinctive Sterling logo are registered trademarks of
Sterling Publishing Co., Inc.

Library of Congress Cataloging-in-Publication Data
Culler, Jonathan D.
  Literary theory / Jonathan Culler.
    p. cm. — (A brief insight)
  Includes bibliographical references and index.
  ISBN 978-1-4027-6875-0
  1. Criticism—History—Handbooks, manuals, etc. 2.
Literature—History and criticism—Theory, etc.—Handbooks, manuals, etc. I. Title.
  PN86.C86 2009
  801'.9509—dc22

                                                                2009013952

10 9 8 7 6 5 4 3 2 1

Published by Sterling Publishing Co., Inc.
387 Park Avenue South, New York, NY 10016

Published by arrangement with Oxford University Press, Inc.

© 1997 Jonathan Culler
Illustrated edition published in 2009 by Sterling Publishing Co., Inc.
Additional text © 2009 Sterling Publishing Co., Inc.

Distributed in Canada by Sterling Publishing
c/o Canadian Manda Group, 165 Dufferin Street
Toronto, Ontario, Canada M6K 3H6

Book design and layout: The DesignWorks Group

Please see picture credits on page 194 for image copyright information.

Sterling ISBN 978-1-4027-6875-0

For information about custom editions, special sales, premium and corporate purchases, please contact
Sterling Special Sales Department at 800-805-5489 or specialsales@sterlingpublishing.com.

CONTENTS

•

PREFACE

•

MANY INTRODUCTIONS TO LITERARY THEORY describe a series of "schools" of criticism. Theory is treated as a series of competing "approaches," each with its theoretical positions and commitments. But the theoretical movements that introductions identify—such as structuralism, deconstruction, feminism, psychoanalysis, Marxism, and new historicism—have a lot in common. This is why people talk about "theory" and not just about particular theories. To introduce theory, it is better to discuss shared questions and claims than to survey theoretical schools. It is preferable to discuss important debates that do not oppose one "school" to another but may mark salient divisions within movements. Treating contemporary theory as a set of competing approaches or methods of interpretation misses much of its interest and force, which come from its broad challenge to common sense, and from its explorations of how meaning is created and human identities take shape. I have preferred to take up a series of topics, focusing on important issues and debates about them and on what I think has been learned.

Still, anyone reading an introductory book on literary theory has a right to expect an explanation of terms such as *structuralism* and *deconstruction*. I offer brief sketches of major critical schools or movements in the Appendix, which can be read first or last or referred to constantly. Enjoy!

ACKNOWLEDGMENTS

•

THIS BOOK OWES MUCH TO STUDENTS in my introductory courses on literary theory at Cornell University, whose questions and arguments over the years have given me a sense of what to say in an introduction. I take special pleasure in thanking Cynthia Chase, Mieke Bal, and Richard Klein, who read and commented on this manuscript, prompting me to rethink and rewrite. Robert Baker, Leland Deladurantaye, and Meg Wesling assisted in particular ways, and Ewa Badowska, who has helped me teach literary theory, made crucial contributions to numerous aspects of this project.

ONE

What Is Theory?

●

IN LITERARY AND CULTURAL STUDIES these days there is a lot of talk about theory—not theory of literature, mind you; just plain "theory." To anyone outside the field, this usage must seem very odd. "Theory of what?" you want to ask. It's surprisingly hard to say. It is not the theory of anything in particular, nor a comprehensive theory of things in general. Sometimes theory seems less an account of anything than an activity—something you do or don't do. You can be involved with theory; you can teach or study theory; you can hate theory or be afraid of it. None of this, though, helps much to understand what theory is.

"Theory," we are told, has radically changed the nature of literary studies, but people who say this do not mean *literary theory*, the systematic account of the nature of literature and of the methods for analyzing it.

Theory in literary studies encompasses multiple fields of inquiry, including psychoanalysis, politics, and philosophy, and encourages a flexible interpretation of nonliterary texts as worthy of literary analysis.

When people complain that there is too much theory in literary studies these days, they don't mean too much systematic reflection on the nature of literature or debate about the distinctive qualities of literary language, for example. Far from it. They have something else in view.

What they have in mind may be precisely that there is too much discussion of nonliterary matters, too much debate about general questions whose relation to literature is scarcely evident, too much reading of difficult psychoanalytical, political, and philosophical texts. Theory is a bunch of (mostly foreign) names; it means Jacques Derrida, Michel Foucault, Luce Irigaray, Jacques Lacan, Judith Butler, Louis Althusser, Gayatri Spivak, for instance.

The Term *Theory*

So what is theory? Part of the problem lies in the term *theory* itself, which gestures in two directions. On the one hand, we speak of "the theory of relativity," for example, an established set of propositions. On the other hand, there is the most ordinary use of the word *theory*.

> "Why did Laura and Michael split up?"
> "Well, my theory is that . . ."

What does *theory* mean here? First, *theory* signals "speculation." But a theory is not the same as a guess. "My guess is that . . ." would suggest that there is a right answer, which I don't happen to know: "My guess is that Laura just got tired of Michael's carping, but we'll find out for sure when their friend Mary gets here." A theory, by contrast, is speculation that might not be affected by what Mary says, an explanation whose truth or falsity might be hard to demonstrate.

"My theory is that . . ." also claims to offer an explanation that is not obvious. We don't expect the speaker to continue, "My theory is that it's because Michael was having an affair with Samantha." That wouldn't count as a theory. It hardly requires theoretical acumen to conclude that if Michael and Samantha were having an affair, that might have had some bearing on Laura's attitude toward Michael. Interestingly, if the speaker *were* to say, "My theory is that Michael was having an affair with Samantha," suddenly the existence of this affair becomes a matter of conjecture, no longer certain, and thus a possible theory. But generally, to count as a theory, not only must an explanation not be obvious; it should involve a certain complexity: "My theory is that Laura was always secretly in love with her father and that Michael could never succeed in becoming the right person." A theory must be more than a hypothesis: it can't be obvious; it involves complex relations of a systematic kind among a number of factors; and it is not easily confirmed or disproved. If we bear these factors in mind, it becomes easier to understand what goes by the name of "theory."

Theory as Genre

Theory in literary studies is not an account of the nature of literature or methods for its study (though such matters are part of theory and will be treated here, primarily in Chapters 2, 5, and 6). It's a body of thinking and writing whose limits are exceedingly hard to define. The philosopher Richard Rorty speaks of a new, mixed genre that began in the nineteenth century: "Beginning in the days of Goethe and Macaulay and Carlyle and Emerson, a new kind of writing has developed which is neither the evaluation of the relative merits of literary productions, nor intellectual history, nor moral philosophy, nor social prophecy, but all of these mingled together in a new genre." The most convenient designation of this miscellaneous genre is simply the nickname *theory*, which has come to designate works that succeed in challenging and reorienting thinking in fields other than those to which they apparently belong. This is the simplest explanation of what makes something count as theory. Works regarded as theory *have* effects beyond their original field.

This simple explanation is an unsatisfactory definition but it does seem to capture what has happened since the 1960s: writings from outside the field of literary studies have been taken up by people in literary studies because their analyses of language, or mind, or history, or culture, offer new and persuasive accounts of textual and cultural matters. Theory in this sense is not a set of methods for literary study but an unbounded group of writings about everything under the sun, from the most technical problems of academic philosophy to the changing ways in which people have talked about and thought about the body. The genre of "theory" includes works of anthropology, art history, film studies, gender studies, linguistics, philosophy, political theory, psychoanalysis, science studies, social and intellectual history, and sociology. The works in question are tied to arguments in these fields, but they become "theory" because their

U.S. philosopher Richard Rorty claims that beginning with the works of such luminaries as German writer, thinker, and dramatist Johann Wolfgang von Goethe, whose statue appears in front of the old stock exchange in Leipzig, there arose a mixed genre of writing that today we call literary theory—a combination of several different disciplines, including literary productions, intellectual history, moral philosophy, and social prophecy.

visions or arguments have been suggestive or productive for people who are not studying those disciplines. Works that become "theory" offer accounts others can use about meaning, nature and culture, the functioning of the psyche, the relations of public to private experience and of larger historical forces to individual experience.

Theory's Effects

If theory is defined by its practical effects, as what changes people's views, makes them think differently about their objects of study and their activities of studying them, what sort of effects are these?

The main effect of theory is the disputing of "common sense": commonsense views about meaning, writing, literature, experience. For example, theory questions

- the conception that the meaning of an utterance or text is what the speaker "had in mind,"
- or the idea that writing is an expression whose truth lies elsewhere, in an experience or a state of affairs which it expresses,
- or the notion that reality is what is "present" at a given moment.

Theory is often a pugnacious critique of commonsense notions, and further, an attempt to show that what we take for granted as "common sense" is in fact a historical construction, a particular theory that has come to seem so natural to us that we don't even see it as a theory. As a critique of common sense and exploration of alternative conceptions, theory involves a questioning of the most basic premises or assumptions of literary study, the unsettling of anything that might have been taken for granted: what is meaning? What is an author? What is it to read? What is the "I" or subject who writes, reads, or acts? How do texts relate to the circumstances in which they are produced?

What is an example of some "theory"? Instead of talking about theory in general, let us plunge right into some difficult writing by two of the most celebrated theorists to see what we can make of it. I propose two related but contrasting cases, which involve critiques of commonsense ideas about "sex," "writing," and "experience."

Foucault on Sex

In his book *The History of Sexuality*, the French intellectual historian Michel Foucault considers what he calls "the repressive hypothesis": the common idea that sex is something that earlier periods, particularly the nineteenth century, have repressed and that moderns have fought to liberate. Far from being something natural that was repressed, Foucault suggests, "sex" is a complex idea produced by a range of social practices, investigations, talk, and writing—"discourses" or "discursive practices" for short—that come together in the nineteenth century. All the sorts of talk—by doctors, clergy, novelists, psychologists, moralists, social workers, politicians—that we link with the idea of the repression of sexuality were in fact ways of bringing into being the thing we call "sex." Foucault writes, "The notion of 'sex' made it possible to group together, in an artificial unity, anatomical elements, biological functions, conducts, sensations, pleasures; and it enabled one to make use of this fictitious unity as a causal principle, an omnipresent meaning, a secret to be discovered everywhere." Foucault is not denying that there are physical acts of sexual intercourse, or that humans have a biological sex and sexual organs. He is claiming that the nineteenth century found new ways of grouping together under a single category ("sex") a range of things that are potentially quite different: certain acts, which we

Is the concept of sex natural? Is it a given? Twentieth-century French philosopher, historian, and celebrated theorist Michel Foucault, shown in a 1976 photo, thought not. In *The History of Sexuality* he posited instead that it was the product of social practices, investigations, and different types of writing and discussions.

call sexual, biological distinctions, parts of bodies, psychological reactions, and, above all, social meanings. People's ways of talking about and dealing with these conducts, sensations, and biological functions created something different, an artificial unity, called "sex," which came to be treated as fundamental to the identity of the individual. Then, by a crucial reversal, this thing called "sex" was seen as the *cause* of the variety of phenomena that had been grouped together to create the idea. This process gave sexuality a new importance and a new role, making sexuality the secret of the individual's nature. Speaking of the importance of the "sexual urge" and our "sexual nature," Foucault notes that we have reached the point

> where we expect our intelligibility to come from what was for many
> centuries thought of as madness, . . . our identity from what was
> perceived as a nameless urge. Hence the importance we ascribe to

it, the reverential fear with which we surround it, the care we take to know it. Hence the fact that over the centuries it has become more important to us than our soul.

One illustration of the way sex was made the secret of the individual's being, a key source of the individual's identity, is the creation in the nineteenth century of "the homosexual" as a type, almost a "species." Earlier periods had stigmatized acts of sexual intercourse between individuals of the same sex (such as sodomy), but now it became a question not of acts but of identity, not of whether someone had performed forbidden actions but of whether he "was" a homosexual. Sodomy was an act, Foucault writes, but "the homosexual was now a species." Previously there were homosexual acts in which people might engage; now it was a question, rather, of a sexual core or essence thought to determine the very being of the individual: is he *a* homosexual?

In Foucault's account, "sex" is constructed by the discourses linked with various social practices and institutions: the way in which doctors, clergy, public officials, social workers, and even novelists treat phenomena they identify as sexual. But these discourses represent sex as something prior to the discourses themselves. Moderns have largely accepted this picture and accused these discourses and social practices of trying to control and repress the sex they are in fact constructing. Reversing this process, Foucault's analysis treats sex as an effect rather than a cause, the product of discourses which attempt to analyze, describe, and regulate the activities of human beings.

Foucault's analysis is an example of an argument from the field of history that has become "theory" because it has inspired and been taken up by people in other fields. It is not a theory of sexuality in the sense of a set of axioms purported to be universal. It claims to be an analysis of a particular historical development, but it clearly has broader implications. It encourages you to be suspicious of what is identified as natural, as a given. Might it not, on the contrary, have been produced by the discourses of experts, by the practices linked with discourses of knowledge that claim to describe it? In Foucault's account, it is the attempt to know the truth about human beings that has produced "sex" as the secret of human nature.

Theory's Moves

A characteristic of thinking that becomes theory is that it offers striking "moves" that people can use in thinking about other topics. One such move is Foucault's suggestion that the supposed opposition between a natural sexuality and the social forces ("power") that repress it might be, rather, a relationship of complicity: social forces bring into being the thing ("sex") they apparently work to control. A further move—a bonus, if you will—is to ask what is achieved by the *concealment* of this complicity between power and the sex it is said to repress. What is achieved when this interdependency is seen as an opposition rather than interdependency? The answer Foucault gives is that this masks the pervasiveness of power: you think that you are resisting power by championing sex, when in fact you are working entirely in the terms that power has set. To put this another way, insofar as this thing called "sex" appears to lie outside power—as something social forces try in vain to control—power looks limited, not very powerful at all (it can't tame sex). In fact, though, power is pervasive; it is everywhere.

Power, for Foucault, is not something someone wields but "power/knowledge": power in the form of knowledge or knowledge as power. What we think we know about the world—the conceptual framework in which we are brought to think about the world—exercises great power. Power/knowledge has produced, for example, the situation where you are defined by your sex. It has produced the situation that defines a woman as someone whose fulfillment as a person is supposed to lie in a sexual relationship with a man. The idea that sex lies outside and in opposition to power conceals the reach of power/knowledge.

There are several important things to note about this example of theory. Theory here in Foucault is analytical—the analysis of a concept—but also inherently speculative in the sense that there is no evidence you could cite to show that this is the correct hypothesis about sexuality. (There is a lot of evidence that makes his account plausible but no decisive test.) Foucault calls this kind of inquiry a "genealogical" critique: an exposure of how supposedly basic categories, such as "sex," are produced by discursive practices. Such a critique does not try to tell us what sex "really" is but seeks to show how the notion has been created. Note also that Foucault here does not speak of literature at all, though this theory has proved to be of great interest to people studying literature. For one thing, literature is about sex; literature is one of the places where this idea of sex is constructed, where we find promoted the idea that people's deepest identities are tied to the kind of desire they feel for another human being. Foucault's account has been important for people studying the novel as well as for those working in gay and lesbian studies and in gender studies in general. Foucault has been especially influential as the inventor of new historical objects: things such as "sex," "punishment," and "madness," which we had not previously thought of as having a history. His works treat such things as historical constructions and thus encourage us to look at how the discursive practices of a period, including literature, may have shaped things we take for granted.

Derrida on Writing

For a second example of "theory"—as influential as Foucault's revision of the history of sexuality but with features that illustrate some differences within "theory"—we might look at an analysis by the contemporary French philosopher Jacques Derrida of a discussion of writing and experience in the *Confessions* of Jean-Jacques Rousseau. Rousseau is a writer of the French eighteenth century often credited with helping to bring into being the modern notion of the individual self.

But first, a bit of background. Traditionally, Western philosophy has distinguished "reality" from "appearance," *things* themselves from *representations* of them, and *thought* from *signs* that express it. Signs or representations, in this view, are but a way to get at reality, truth, or ideas, and they should be as transparent as possible; they should not get in the way, should not affect or infect the thought or truth they represent. In this framework, speech has seemed the immediate manifestation or presence of thought, while writing, which operates in the absence of the speaker, has been treated as an artificial and derivative representation of speech, a potentially misleading sign of a sign.

Rousseau follows this tradition, which has passed into common sense, when he writes, "Languages are made to be spoken; writing serves only as a supplement to speech." Here Derrida intervenes, asking "What is a supplement?" Webster's defines *supplement* as "something that completes or makes an addition." Does writing "complete" speech by supplying something essential that was missing, or does it add something that speech could perfectly well do without? Rousseau repeatedly characterizes writing as a mere addition, an inessential extra, even "a disease of speech": writing consists of signs that introduce the possibility of misunderstanding since they are read in the absence of the speaker, who is not there to explain or correct.

But though Rousseau calls writing an inessential extra, his works in fact treat it as what completes or makes up for something lacking in speech: writing is repeatedly brought in to compensate for the flaws in speech, such as the possibility of misunderstanding. For instance, Rousseau writes in his *Confessions*, which inaugurates the notion of the self as an "inner" reality unknown to society, that he has chosen to write his *Confessions* and to hide himself from society because in society he would show himself "not just at a disadvantage but as completely different from what I am. . . . If I were present people would never have known what I was worth." For Rousseau, then, his "true" inner self is different from the self that appears in conversations with others, and he needs writing to supplement the misleading signs of his speech. Writing turns out to be essential because speech has qualities previously attributed to writing: like writing, it consists of signs that are not transparent, do not automatically convey the meaning intended by the speaker, but are open to interpretation.

Writing is a supplement to speech but speech is already a supplement: children, Rousseau writes, quickly learn to use speech "to supplement their own weakness . . . for it does not need much experience to realize how pleasant it is to act through the hands of others and to move the world simply by moving the tongue." In a move characteristic of theory, Derrida treats this particular case as an instance of a common structure or a logic: a "logic of supplementarity" that he discovers in Rousseau's works. This logic is a structure where the thing supplemented (speech) turns out to need supplementation because it proves to have the same qualities originally thought to characterize only the supplement (writing). I shall try to explain.

Rousseau needs writing because speech gets misinterpreted. More generally, he needs signs because things themselves don't satisfy. In the

Confessions Rousseau describes his love as an adolescent for Madame de Warens, in whose house he lived and whom he called "Maman."

Jean-Jacques Rousseau's *Confessions* is one of the most famous autobiographies ever written. Describing his adolescent love for his benefactor Madame de Warens, the eighteenth-century French philosopher and writer, pictured in a work by Scottish painter Allan Ramsay, explained that to convey his true self he needed writing to supplement speech.

I would never finish if I were to describe in detail all the follies that the recollection of my dear Maman made me commit when I was no longer in her presence. How often I kissed my bed, recalling that she had slept in it, my curtains and all the furniture in the room, since they belonged to her and her beautiful hand had touched them, even the floor, on which I prostrated myself, thinking that she had walked upon it.

These different objects function in her absence as supplements or substitutes for her presence. But it turns out that even in her presence the same structure, the same need for supplements, persists. Rousseau continues,

Sometimes even in her presence I committed extravagances that only the most violent love seemed capable of inspiring. One day at table, just as she had put a piece of food into her mouth, I exclaimed that I saw a hair on it. She put the morsel back on her plate; I eagerly seized and swallowed it.

Her absence, when he has to make do with substitutes or signs that recall her to him, is first contrasted with her presence. But it turns out that her presence is not a moment of fulfillment, of immediate access to the thing itself, without supplements or signs; in her presence too the structure, the need for supplements is the same. Hence the grotesque incident of swallowing the food she had put into her mouth. And the chain of substitutions can be continued. Even if Rousseau were to "possess her," as we say, he would still feel that she escaped him and could only be anticipated and recalled. And "Maman" herself is a substitute for the mother Rousseau never knew—a mother who would not have sufficed but who would, like all mothers, have failed to satisfy and have required supplements.

"Through this series of supplements," Derrida writes, "there emerges a law: that of an endless linked series, ineluctably multiplying the supplementary mediations that produce the sense of the very thing that they defer: the impression of the thing itself, of immediate presence, or originary perception. Immediacy is derived. Everything begins with the intermediary." The more these texts want to tell us of the importance of the presence of the thing itself, the more they show the necessity of intermediaries. These signs or supplements are in fact responsible for the sense that there is something there (like Maman) to grasp. What we learn from these texts is that the idea of the original is created by the copies, and that the original is always deferred—never to be grasped. The conclusion is that our commonsense notion of reality as something present, and of the original as something that was once present, proves untenable: experience is always mediated by signs and the "original" is produced as an effect of signs, of supplements.

For Derrida, Rousseau's texts, like many others, propose that instead of thinking of life as something to which signs and texts are added to represent it, we should conceive of life itself as suffused with signs, made what it is by processes of signification. Writings may claim that reality is prior to signification, but in fact they show that, in a famous phrase of Derrida's, "Il n'y a pas de hors-texte"—"There is no outside-of-text": when you think you are getting outside signs and text, to "reality itself," what you find is more text, more signs, chains of supplements. Derrida writes,

> What we have tried to show in following the connecting thread of
> the "dangerous supplement" is that in what we call the real life of

these "flesh and blood" creatures, . . . there has never been anything but writing, there have never been anything but supplements and substitutional significations which could only arise in a chain of differential relations. . . . And so on indefinitely, for we have read *in the text* that the absolute present, Nature, what is named by words like "real mother," etc. have always already escaped, have never existed; that what inaugurates meaning and language is writing as the disappearance of natural presence.

This does not mean that there is no difference between the presence of "Maman" and her absence or between a "real" event and a fictional one. It's that her presence turns out to be a particular kind of absence, still requiring mediations and supplements.

What the Examples Show

Foucault and Derrida are often grouped together as "post-structuralists" (see Appendix), but these two examples of "theory" present striking differences. Derrida's offers a reading or interpretation of texts, identifying a logic at work in a text. Foucault's claim is not based on texts—in fact he cites amazingly few actual documents or discourses—but offers a general framework for thinking about texts and discourses in general. Derrida's interpretation shows the extent to which literary works themselves, such as Rousseau's *Confessions*, are theoretical: they offer explicit speculative arguments about writing, desire, and substitution or supplementation, and they guide thinking about these topics in ways that they leave implicit. Foucault, on the other hand, proposes to show us not how insightful or

Image of a bookplate by the engraver Sidney Lawton Smith.

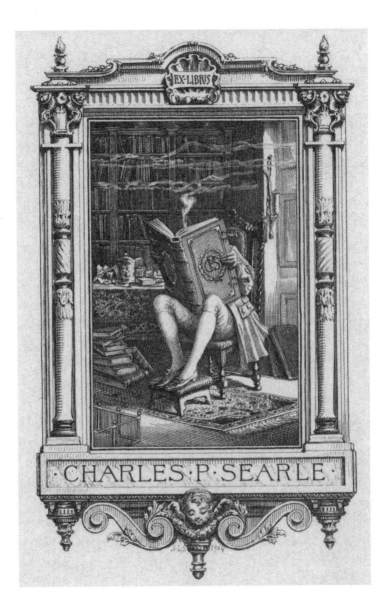

wise texts are but how far the discourses of doctors, scientists, novelists, and others create the things they claim only to analyze. Derrida shows how theoretical the literary works are, Foucault how creatively productive the discourses of knowledge are.

There also seems to be a difference in what they are claiming and what questions arise. Derrida is claiming to tell us what Rousseau's texts say or show, so the question that arises is whether what Rousseau's texts say is true. Foucault claims to analyze a particular historical moment, so the question that arises is whether his large generalizations hold for other times and places. Raising follow-up questions like these is, in turn, our way of stepping into "theory" and practicing it.

Both examples of theory illustrate that theory involves speculative practice: accounts of desire, language, and so on, that challenge received ideas (that there is something natural, called "sex"; that signs represent prior realities). So doing, they incite you to rethink the categories with which you may be reflecting on literature. These examples display the main thrust of recent theory, which has been the critique of whatever is taken as natural, the demonstration that what has been thought or declared natural is in fact a historical, cultural product. What happens can be grasped through a different example: when Aretha Franklin sings "You make me feel like a natural woman," she seems happy to be confirmed in a "natural" sexual identity, prior to culture, by a man's treatment of her. But her formulation, "you make me feel *like* a natural woman," suggests that the supposedly natural or given identity is a cultural role, an effect that has been produced within culture: she *isn't* a "natural woman" but has to be made to feel *like* one. The natural woman is a cultural product.

Theory makes other arguments analogous to this one, whether maintaining that apparently natural social arrangements and institutions, and also the habits of thought of a society, are the product of underlying economic relations and ongoing power struggles, or that the phenomena of conscious life may be produced by unconscious forces, or that what we call the self or subject is produced in and through the systems of language and culture, or that what we call "presence," "origin," or the "original" is created by copies, an effect of repetition.

So what is theory? Four main points have emerged.

1. Theory is interdisciplinary—discourse with effects outside an original discipline.
2. Theory is analytical and speculative—an attempt to work out what is involved in what we call sex or language or writing or meaning or the subject.
3. Theory is a critique of common sense, of concepts taken as natural.
4. Theory is reflexive, thinking about thinking, inquiry into the categories we use in making sense of things, in literature and in other discursive practices.

As a result, theory is intimidating. One of the most dismaying features of theory today is that it is endless. It is not something that you could ever master, not a particular group of texts you could learn so as to "know theory." It is an unbounded corpus of writings which is always being augmented as the young and the restless, in critiques of the guiding conceptions of their elders, promote the contributions to theory of new thinkers and rediscover the work of older, neglected ones. Theory is thus a source of intimidation, a resource for constant upstagings: "What? You haven't read Lacan! How can you talk about the lyric without addressing the specular constitution of the speaking subject?" Or "How can you write about the Victorian novel without using Foucault's account of the deployment of sexuality and the hysterization of women's bodies and Gayatri Spivak's demonstration of the role of colonialism in the construction of the metropolitan subject?" At times, theory presents itself as a diabolical sentence condemning you to hard reading in unfamiliar fields, where even the completion of one task will bring not respite but further difficult assignments. ("Spivak? Yes, but have you read Benita Parry's critique of Spivak and her response?")

The unmasterability of theory is a major cause of resistance to it. No matter how well versed you may think yourself, you can never be sure whether you "have to read" Jean Baudrillard, Mikhail Bakhtin, Walter Benjamin, Hélène Cixous, C. L. R. James, Melanie Klein, or Julia Kristeva, or whether you can "safely" forget them. (It will, of course, depend on who "you" are and who you want to be.) A good deal of the hostility to theory no doubt comes from the fact that to admit the importance of theory is to make an open-ended commitment, to leave yourself in a position where there are always important things you don't know. But this is the condition of life itself.

Theory makes you desire mastery: you hope that theoretical reading will give you the concepts to organize and understand the phenomena that concern you. But theory makes mastery impossible, not only because there is always more to know, but, more specifically and more painfully, because theory is itself the questioning of presumed results and the assumptions on which they are based. The nature of theory is to undo, through a contesting of premises and postulates, what you thought you knew, so the effects of theory are not predictable. You have not become master, but neither are you where you were before. You reflect on your reading in new ways. You have different questions to ask and a better sense of the implications of the questions you put to works you read.

This introduction will not make you a master of theory, and not just because it is short, but it outlines significant lines of thought and areas of debate, especially those pertaining to literature. It presents examples of theoretical investigation in the hope that readers will find theory valuable and engaging and take occasion to sample the pleasures of thought.

TWO

What Is Literature and
Does It Matter?

•

WHAT IS LITERATURE? You'd think this would be a central question for literary theory, but in fact it has not seemed to matter very much. Why should this be?

There appear to be two main reasons. First, since theory itself intermingles ideas from philosophy, linguistics, history, political theory, and psychoanalysis, why should theorists worry about whether the texts they're reading are literary or not? For students and teachers of literature today there is a whole range of critical projects, topics to read and write about—such as "images of women in the early twentieth century"—

The literary logic of storytelling is in fact essential to nonliterary fields as well. Historians attempt to show how one event led to another—for instance, how the 1914 assassination of Archduke Franz Ferdinand of Austria in Sarajevo led to World War I. Ferdinand and his wife, Sophie, Duchess of Hohenberg, who was killed at the same time as her husband, are shown here in an undated photograph.

where you can deal with both literary and nonliterary works. You can study Virginia Woolf's novels or Freud's case histories or both, and the distinction doesn't seem methodologically crucial. It's not that all texts are somehow equal: some texts are taken to be richer, more powerful, more exemplary, more contestatory, more central, for one reason or another. But both literary and nonliterary works can be studied together and in similar ways.

Literariness Outside Literature

Second, the distinction has not seemed central because works of theory have discovered what is most simply called the "literariness" of nonliterary phenomena. Qualities often thought to be literary turn out to be crucial to nonliterary discourses and practices as well. For instance, discussions of the nature of historical understanding have taken as a model what is involved in understanding a story. Characteristically, historians do not produce explanations that are like the predictive explanations of science: they cannot show that when x and y occur, z will necessarily happen. What they do, rather, is to show how one thing led to another, how the First World War *came to* break out, not why it *had* to happen. The model for historical explanation is thus the logic of stories: the way a story shows how something came to happen, connecting the initial situation, the development, and the outcome in a way that makes sense.

The model for historical intelligibility, in short, is literary narrative. We who hear and read stories are good at telling whether a plot makes sense, hangs together, or whether the story remains unfinished. If the same models of what makes sense and what counts as a story characterize both literary and historical narratives, then distinguishing between them need not seem an urgent theoretical matter. Similarly, theorists have come to

The novels of British writer Virginia Woolf (depicted here in a 1928 photograph) and the case histories of neurologist and psychoanalyst Sigmund Freud (whose analytic couch is shown in this image from the Freud Museum in London) both provide images of women in the early twentieth century.

insist on the importance in nonliterary texts—whether Freud's accounts of his psychoanalytic cases or works of philosophical argument—of rhetorical devices such as metaphor, which have been thought crucial to literature but have often been considered purely ornamental in other sorts of discourses. In showing how rhetorical figures shape thought in other discourses as well, theorists demonstrate a powerful literariness at work in supposedly nonliterary texts, thus complicating the distinction between the literary and the nonliterary.

But the fact that I describe this situation by speaking of the discovery of the "literariness" of nonliterary phenomena indicates that the notion of literature continues to play a role and needs to be addressed.

What Sort of Question?

We find ourselves back at the key question, "What is literature?," which will not go away. But what sort of question is it? If a five-year-old is asking, it's easy. "Literature," you answer, "is stories, poems, and plays." But if the questioner is a literary theorist, it's harder to know how to take the query. It might be a question about the general nature of this object, literature, which both of you already know well. What sort of object or activity is it? What does it do? What purposes does it serve? Thus understood, "What is literature?" asks not for a definition but for an analysis, even an argument about why one might concern oneself with literature at all.

But "What is literature?" might also be a question about distinguishing characteristics of the works known as literature: what distinguishes them from nonliterary works? What differentiates literature from other human activities or pastimes? Now people might ask this question because they were wondering how to decide which books are literature and which are not, but it is more likely that they already have an idea what counts as literature and want to know something else: are there any essential, distinguishing features that literary works share?

This is a difficult question. Theorists have wrestled with it, but without notable success. The reasons are not far to seek: works of literature come in all shapes and sizes and most of them seem to have more in common with works that aren't usually called literature than they do with some other works recognized as literature. Charlotte Brontë's *Jane Eyre*, for instance, more closely resembles an autobiography than it does a sonnet, and a poem by Robert Burns—"My love is like a red, red rose"—resembles a folk song

Charlotte Brontë's *Jane Eyre,* Robert Burns's poetry, Shakespeare's *Hamlet*: Do novels, poems, and plays share features that distinguish them from other works, such as songs, transcribed conversations, and autobiographies?

more than it does Shakespeare's *Hamlet*. Are there qualities shared by poems, plays, and novels that distinguish them from, say, songs, transcriptions of conversations, and autobiographies?

Historical Variations

Even a bit of historical perspective makes this question more complex. For twenty-five centuries people have written works that we call literature today, but the modern sense of *literature* is scarcely two centuries old. Prior to 1800, *literature* and analogous terms in other European languages meant "writings" or "book knowledge." Even today, a scientist who says "the literature on evolution is immense" means not that many poems and novels treat the topic but that much has been written about it. And works that today are studied as literature in English or Latin classes in schools and universities were once treated not as a special kind of writing but as fine examples of the use of language and rhetoric. They were instances of a larger category of exemplary practices of writing and thinking, which included speeches, sermons, history, and philosophy. Students were not asked to interpret them, as we now interpret literary works, seeking to explain what they are "really about." On the contrary, students memorized them, studied their grammar, identified their rhetorical figures and their structures or procedures of argument. A work such as Virgil's *Aeneid*, which today is studied as literature, was treated very differently in schools prior to 1850.

The modern Western sense of literature as imaginative writing can be traced to the German Romantic theorists of the late eighteenth century and, if we want a particular source, to a book published in 1800 by a French baroness, Madame de Staël's *On Literature Considered in Its Relations with Social Institutions*. But even if we restrict ourselves to the last two

Before 1850, students memorized and analyzed the grammar and arguments of works such as Virgil's *Aeneid*, which today we read and interpret as literature. This detail from a 1603 landscape oil painting by Dutch artist Frederick van Valckenborch shows scenes from the epic poem.

centuries, the category of literature becomes slippery: would works which today count as literature—say poems that seem snippets of ordinary conversation, without rhyme or discernible metre—have qualified as literature for Madame de Staël? And once we begin to think about non-European cultures, the question of what counts as literature becomes increasingly difficult. It is tempting to give it up and conclude that literature is whatever a given society treats as literature—a set of texts that cultural arbiters recognize as belonging to literature.

Such a conclusion is completely unsatisfying, of course. It simply displaces instead of resolving the question: rather than ask "What is literature?" we need to ask "What makes us (or some other society) treat

French baroness and author Madame de Staël (1766–1817) traveled throughout Germany and wrote as a result *De l'Allemagne* (1810), the whole first edition of which was declared "un-French" and ordered destroyed by Napoleon. Her *On Literature Considered in Its Relations with Social Institutions*, to which we attribute the modern Western sense of literature as imaginative writing, was published in 1810.

something as literature?" There are, though, other categories that work in this way, referring not to specific properties but only to changing criteria of social groups. Take the question "What is a weed?" Is there an essence of "weedness"—a special something, a *je ne sais quoi*, that weeds share and that distinguishes them from nonweeds? Anyone who has been enlisted to help weed a garden knows how hard it is to tell a weed from a nonweed and may wonder whether there is a secret. What would it be? How do you recognize a weed? Well, the secret is that there isn't a secret. Weeds are simply plants that gardeners don't want to have growing in their gardens. If you were curious about weeds, seeking the nature of "weedness," it would be a waste of time to try to investigate their botanical nature, to seek distinctive formal or physical qualities that make plants weeds. You would have to carry out instead historical, sociological, perhaps psychological inquiries about the sorts of plants that are judged undesirable by different groups in different places.

Perhaps *literature* is like *weed*.

But this answer doesn't eliminate the question. It changes it to "What is involved in treating things *as* literature in our culture?"

Treating Texts as Literature

Suppose you come across the following sentence:

> *We dance round in a ring and suppose,*
> *But the Secret sits in the middle and knows.*

What is this, and how do you know?

Well, it matters a good deal *where* you come across it. If this sentence is printed on a slip in a Chinese fortune cookie, you may well take it as an unusually enigmatical fortune, but when it is offered (as it is here) as an example, you cast around for possibilities among uses of language familiar to you. Is it a riddle, asking us to guess the secret? Might it be an advertisement for something called "Secret"? Ads often rhyme— "Winston tastes good, like a cigarette should"—and they have grown increasingly enigmatic in their attempts to jostle a jaded public. But this sentence seems detached from any readily imaginable practical context, including that of selling a product. This, and the fact that it rhymes and, after the first two words, follows a regular rhythm of alternating stressed and unstressed syllables ("róund in a ríng and suppóse") creates the possibility that this might be poetry, an instance of literature.

There is a puzzle here, though: the fact that this sentence has no obvious practical import is what mainly creates the possibility that it might be literature, but could we not achieve that effect by lifting other sentences out of the contexts that make it clear what they do? Suppose we take a sentence out of an instruction booklet, a recipe, an advertisement, a newspaper, and set it down on a page in isolation:

Stir vigorously and allow to sit five minutes.

Is this literature? Have I made it literature by extracting it from the practical context of a recipe? Perhaps, but it is scarcely clear that I have. Something seems lacking; the sentence seems not to have the resources for you to work with. To make it literature you need, perhaps, to imagine a title whose relation to the line would pose a problem and exercise the imagination: for instance, "The Secret," or "The Quality of Mercy."

Something like that would help, but a sentence fragment such as "A sugar plum on a pillow in the morning" seems to have a better chance of becoming literature because its failure to be anything except an image invites a certain kind of attention, calls for reflection. So do sentences where the relation between their form and their content provides potential food for thought. Thus the opening sentence of a book of philosophy, W. O. Quine's *From a Logical Point of View*, might conceivably be a poem:

> A curious thing
> about the ontological problem is its
> simplicity.

Set down in this way on a page, surrounded by intimidating margins of silence, this sentence can attract a certain kind of attention that we might call literary: an interest in the words, their relations to one another, and their implications, and particularly an interest in how what is said relates to the way it is said. That is, set down in this way, this sentence seems able to live up to a certain modern idea of a poem and to respond to a kind of attention that today is associated with literature. If someone were to say this sentence to you, you would ask, "What do you mean?"

but if you take the sentence as a poem, the question isn't quite the same: not what does the speaker or author mean but what does the poem mean? How does this language work? What does this sentence do?

Isolated in the first line, the words "A curious thing" may raise the question of what is a thing and what is it for a thing to be curious. "What is a thing?" is one of the problems of ontology, the science of being or study of what exists. But "thing" in the phrase "a curious thing" is not a physical object but something like a relation or aspect which doesn't seem to exist in the same way that a stone or a house does. The sentence preaches simplicity but seems not to practice what it preaches, illustrating, in the ambiguities of *thing*, something of the forbidding complexities of ontology. But perhaps the very simplicity of the poem—the fact that it stops after "simplicity," as if no more need be said—gives some credibility to the implausible assertion of simplicity. At any rate, isolated in this way, the sentence can give rise to the sort of activity of interpretation associated with literature—the sort of activity I have been carrying out here.

What can such thought experiments tell us about literature? They suggest, first of all, that when language is removed from other contexts, detached from other purposes, it can be interpreted as literature (though it must possess some qualities that make it responsive to such interpretation). If literature is language decontextualized, cut off from other functions and purposes, it is also itself a context, which promotes or elicits special kinds of attention. For instance, readers attend to potential complexities and look for implicit meanings, without assuming, say, that the utterance is telling them to do something. To describe "literature" would be to analyze a set of assumptions and interpretive operations readers may bring to bear on such texts.

Conventions of Literature

One relevant convention or disposition that has emerged from the analysis of stories (ranging from personal anecdotes to entire novels) goes by the forbidding name of the "hyper-protected cooperative principle" but is actually rather simple. Communication depends on the basic convention that participants are cooperating with one another and that, therefore, what one person says to the other is likely to be relevant. If I ask you whether George is a good student and you reply, "He is usually punctual," I make sense of your reply by assuming that you are cooperating and saying something relevant to my question. Instead of complaining, "You didn't answer my question," I may conclude that you did answer implicitly and indicated that there's little positive to be said about George as a student. I assume, that is, that you are cooperating unless there is compelling evidence to the contrary.

Now literary narratives can be seen as members of a larger class of stories, "narrative display texts," utterances whose relevance to listeners lies not in information they convey but in their "tellability." Whether you are telling an anecdote to a friend or writing a novel for posterity, you are doing something different from, say, testifying in court: you are trying to produce a story that will seem "worth it" to your listeners: that will have some sort of point or significance, will amuse or give pleasure. What sets off literary works from other narrative display texts is that they have undergone a process of selection: they have been published, reviewed, and reprinted, so that readers approach them with the assurance that others have found them well constructed and "worth it." So for literary works, the cooperative

When we create literature, we are trying to produce a story that will be "worth it"—that will be worth the time and energy it takes the audience to listen to or read the story. In this manuscript illumination from a facsimile of the *Manessa Codex* (ca. 1300), the poet Geoffrey de Strasbourg is shown reciting the tales and heroic legends of Tristan and Iseult.

principle is "hyper-protected." We can put up with many obscurities and apparent irrelevancies, without assuming that this makes no sense. Readers assume that in literature complications of language ultimately have a communicative purpose and, instead of imagining that the speaker or writer is being uncooperative, as they might in other speech contexts, they struggle to interpret elements that flout principles of efficient communication in the interests of some further communicative goal. "Literature" is an institutional label that gives us reason to expect that the results of our reading efforts will be "worth it." And many of the features of literature follow from the willingness of readers to pay attention, to explore uncertainties, and not immediately ask "What do you mean by that?"

Literature, we might conclude, is a speech act or textual event that elicits certain kinds of attention. It contrasts with other sorts of speech acts, such as imparting information, asking questions, or making promises. Most of the time what leads readers to treat something as literature is that they find it in a context that identifies it as literature: in a book of poems or a section of a magazine, library, or bookstore.

A Puzzle

But we have another puzzle here. Aren't there special ways of organizing language that tell us something is literature? Or is the fact that we know something is literature what leads us to give it a kind of attention we don't give newspapers and, as a result, to find in it special kinds of organization and implicit meanings? The answer must surely be that both cases occur: sometimes the object has features that make it literary but sometimes it is the literary context that makes us treat it as literature. But highly organized language doesn't necessarily make something literature: nothing is more highly patterned than the telephone directory. And we can't make just any piece of language literature by calling it literature: I can't pick up my old chemistry textbook and read it as a novel.

On the one hand, "literature" is not just a frame in which we put language: not every sentence will make it as literature if set down on a page as a poem. But, on the other hand, literature is not just a special kind of language, for many literary works don't flaunt their difference from other sorts of language; they function in special ways because of the special attention they receive.

We have a complicated structure here. We are dealing with two different perspectives that overlap, intersect, but don't seem to yield a synthesis. We can think of literary works as language with particular properties or features, and we can think of literature as the product of conventions and a certain kind of attention. Neither perspective successfully incorporates the other, and one must shift back and forth between them. I take up five points theorists have made about the nature of literature: with each, you start from one perspective but must, in the end, make allowance for the other.

The Nature of Literature

1. Literature as the "Foregrounding" of Language

"Literariness" is often said to lie above all in the organization of language that makes literature distinguishable from language used for other purposes. Literature is language that "foregrounds" language itself: makes it strange, thrusts it at you—"Look! I'm language!"—so you can't forget that you are dealing with language shaped in odd ways. In particular, poetry organizes the sound plane of language so as to make it something to reckon with. Here is the beginning of a poem by Gerard Manley Hopkins called "Inversnaid":

This darksome burn, horseback brown,
His rollrock highroad roaring down,
In coop and in coomb the fleece of his foam
Flutes and low to the lake falls home.

The foregrounding of linguistic patterning—the rhythmical repetition of sounds in "burn . . . brown . . . rollrock . . . road roaring"—as well as the unusual verbal combinations such as "rollrock" make it clear that we are dealing with language organized to attract attention to the linguistic structures themselves.

But it is also true that in many cases readers don't notice linguistic patterning unless something is identified as literature. You don't listen when reading standard prose. The rhythm of this sentence, you will find, is scarcely one that strikes the reader's ear; but if a rhyme should suddenly appear, it makes the rhythm something that you hear. The rhyme, a conventional mark of literariness, makes you notice the rhythm that was there all along. When a text is framed as literature, we are disposed to attend to sound patterning or other sorts of linguistic organization we generally ignore.

2. Literature as the Integration of Language

Literature is language in which the various elements and components of the text are brought into a complex relation. When I receive a letter requesting a contribution for some worthy cause, I am unlikely to find that the sound is echo to the sense, but in literature there are relations—of reinforcement or contrast and dissonance—between the structures of different linguistic levels: between sound and meaning, between grammatical organization and thematic patterns. A rhyme, by bringing two words together ("suppose/knows"), brings their meanings into relation (is "knowing" the opposite of "supposing"?).

But it is clear that neither (1) nor (2) nor both together provides a definition of literature. Not all literature foregrounds language as (1) suggests (many novels do not), and language foregrounded is not necessarily literature. Tongue twisters ("Peter Piper picked a peck of pickled peppers") are seldom thought to be literature, though they call attention to themselves as language and trip you up. In advertisements the linguistic devices are often foregrounded even more blatantly than in lyrics and different structural levels may be integrated more imperiously. One eminent theorist, Roman Jakobson, cites as his key example of the "poetic function" of language not a line from a lyric but a political slogan from the American presidential campaign of Dwight D. ("Ike") Eisenhower: *I like Ike*. Here, through word play, the object liked (Ike) and the liking subject (I) are both enveloped in

This September 1952 photograph shows Eisenhower in Baltimore, Maryland, during his presidential campaign, surrounded by "I Like Ike" posters.

the act (like): how could I not like Ike, when *I* and *Ike* are both contained in *like*? Through this ad, the necessity of liking Ike seems inscribed in the very structure of the language. So, it's not that the relations between different levels of language are relevant only in literature but that in literature we are more likely to look for and exploit relations between form and meaning or theme and grammar and, attempting to understand the contribution each element makes to the effect of the whole, find integration, harmony, tension, or dissonance.

Accounts of literariness focused on the foregrounding or on the integration of language don't provide tests by which, say, Martians could separate works of literature from other sorts of writing. Such accounts function, like most claims about the nature of literature, to direct attention to certain aspects of literature which they claim to be central. To study something as literature, this account tells us, is to look above all at the organization of its language, not to read it as the expression of its author's psyche or as the reflection of the society that produced it.

3. Literature as Fiction

One reason why readers attend to literature differently is that its utterances have a special relation to the world—a relation we call "fictional." The literary work is a linguistic event which projects a fictional world that includes speaker, actors, events, and an implied audience (an audience that takes shape through the work's decisions about what must be explained and what the audience is presumed to know). Literary works refer to imaginary rather than historical individuals (Emma Bovary, Huckleberry Finn), but fictionality is not limited to characters and events. Deictics, as they are called, orientational features of language that relate to the situation of utterance, such as pronouns (I, you) or adverbials of place and time (here, there, now, then, yesterday, tomorrow), function in special ways in literature. *Now* in a poem ("now . . . gathering swallows twitter in the skies") refers not to the instant when the poet first wrote down that word, or to the moment of first publication, but to a time in the poem, in the fictional world of its action. And the "I" that appears in a lyric poem, such as Wordsworth's "I wandered lonely as a cloud . . . ," is also fictional; it refers to the speaker of the poem, who may be quite different from the empirical individual, William Wordsworth, who wrote the poem. (There may well be strong connections between what happens to the speaker or narrator of the poem and what happened to Wordsworth at some moment in his life. But a poem written by an old man may have a young speaker and vice versa. And, notoriously, the narrators of novels, the characters who say "I" as they recount the story, may have experiences and make judgments that are quite different from those of their authors.)

In fiction, the relation of what speakers say to what authors think is always a matter of interpretation. So is the relationship between events recounted and situations in the world. Nonfictional discourse is usually embedded in a context that tells you how to take it: an instruction manual, a newspaper report, a letter from a charity. The context of fiction, though, explicitly leaves open the question of what the fiction is really about. Reference to the world is not so much a property of literary works as a function they are given by interpretation. If I tell a friend, "Meet me for dinner at the Hard Rock Café at eight tomorrow," he or she will take this as a concrete invitation and identify spatial and temporal referents from the context of utterance ("tomorrow" means January 14, 2002, "eight" mean 8 p.m. eastern standard time). But when the poet Ben Jonson writes a poem "Inviting a Friend to Supper," the fictionality of this work makes its relation to the world a matter of interpretation: the context of the message is a literary one and we have to decide whether to take the poem as primarily characterizing the attitudes of a fictional speaker, outlining a bygone way of life, or suggesting that friendship and simple pleasures are what is most important to human happiness.

Interpreting *Hamlet* is, among other things, a matter of deciding whether it should be read as talking about, say, the problems of Danish princes, or the dilemmas of men of the Renaissance experiencing changes in the conception of the self, or relations between men and their mothers in general, or the question of how representations (including literary ones) affect the problem of making sense of our experience. The fact that there are references to Denmark throughout the play doesn't mean that you necessarily read it as talking about Denmark; that is an interpretive decision. We can relate *Hamlet* to the world in different ways at several different levels. The fictionality of literature separates language from other contexts in which it might be used and leaves the work's relation to the world open to interpretation.

4. Literature as Aesthetic Object

The features of literature discussed so far—the supplementary levels of linguistic organization, the separation from practical contexts of utterance, the fictional relation to the world—may be brought together under the general heading of the aesthetic function of language. Aesthetics is historically the name for the theory of art and has involved debates about whether beauty is an objective property of works of art or a subjective response of viewers, and about the relation of the beautiful to the true and the good.

For Immanuel Kant, the primary theorist of modern Western aesthetics, the aesthetic is the name of the attempt to bridge the gap between the material and the spiritual world, between a world of forces and magnitudes and a world of concepts. Aesthetic objects, such as paintings or works of literature, with their combination of sensuous form (colors, sounds) and spiritual content (ideas), illustrate the possibility of bringing together the material and the spiritual. A literary work is an aesthetic object because, with other communicative functions initially bracketed or suspended, it engages readers to consider the interrelation between form and content.

Aesthetic objects, for Kant and other theorists, have a "purposiveness without purpose." There is a purposiveness to their construction: they are made so that their parts will work together toward some end. But the end is the work of art itself, pleasure in the work or pleasure occasioned by the work, not some external purpose. Practically, this means that to consider a text as literature is to ask about the contribution of its parts to the effect of the whole but not to take the work as primarily destined to accomplishing some purpose, such as informing or persuading us. When I say that stories are utterances whose relevance is their "tellability," I am noting that there is a purposiveness to stories (qualities that can make them "good stories") but that this cannot easily be attached to some external purpose, and thus am registering the aesthetic, affective quality of stories, even nonliterary ones. A good story is tellable, strikes readers or listeners as "worth it." It may amuse or instruct or incite, can have a range of effects, but you can't define good stories in general as those that do any one of these things.

5. Literature as Intertextual or Self-Reflexive Construct

Recent theorists have argued that works are made out of other works: made possible by prior works which they take up, repeat, challenge, transform.

This notion sometimes goes by the fancy name of "intertextuality." A work exists between and among other texts, through its relations to them. To read something as literature is to consider it as a linguistic event that has meaning in relation to other discourses: for example, as a poem that plays on possibilities created by previous poems or as a novel that puts on stage and criticizes the political rhetoric of its day. Shakespeare's sonnet "My mistress' eyes are nothing like the sun" takes up the metaphors used in the tradition of love poetry and denies them ("But no such roses see I in her cheeks")—denies them as a way of praising a woman who, "when she walks, treads on the ground." The poem has meaning in relation to the tradition that makes it possible.

Now since to read a poem as literature is to relate it to other poems, to compare and contrast the way it makes sense with the ways others do, it is possible to read poems as at some level about poetry itself. They bear on the operations of poetic imagination and poetic interpretation. Here we encounter another notion that has been important in recent theory: that of the "self-reflexivity" of literature. Novels are at some level about novels, about the problems and possibilities of representing and giving shape or meaning to experience. So *Madame Bovary* can be read as an exploration of relations between Emma Bovary's "real life" and the way which both the romantic novels she reads and Flaubert's own novel make sense of experience. One can always ask of a novel (or a poem) how what it implicitly says about making sense relates to the way it itself goes about making sense.

Literature is a practice in which authors attempt to advance or renew literature and thus is always implicitly a reflection on literature itself. But once again, we find that this is something we could say about other forms: bumper stickers, like poems, may depend for their meaning on prior bumper stickers: "Nuke a Whale for Jesus!" makes no sense without "No Nukes," "Save the Whales," and "Jesus Saves," and one could certainly say that "Nuke a Whale for Jesus" is really *about* bumper stickers. The intertextuality and self-reflexivity of literature is not, finally, a defining feature but a foregrounding of aspects of language use and questions about representation that may also be observed elsewhere.

Properties Versus Consequences

In each of these five cases we encounter the structure I mentioned above: we are dealing with what might be described as *properties* of literary works, features that mark them as literature, but with what could also be seen as the results of a particular kind of attention, a function that we accord language in considering it *as* literature. Neither perspective, it seems, can englobe the other to become the comprehensive perspective. The qualities of literature can't be reduced either to objective properties or to consequences of ways of framing language. There is one key reason for this which already emerged from the little thought experiments at the beginning of this chapter. Language resists the frames we impose. It is hard to make the couplet "We dance round in a ring . . ." into a fortune-cookie fortune or "Stir vigorously" into a stirring poem. When we treat something as literature, when we look for pattern and coherence, there is resistance in the language; we have to work on it, work with it. Finally, the "literariness" of literature may lie in the tension of the interaction between the linguistic material and readers' conventional expectations of what literature is. But I say this with caution, for the other thing we have learned from our five cases is that each quality identified as an important feature of literature turns out not to be a *defining* feature, since it can be found at work in other language uses.

The Functions of Literature

I began this chapter by noting that literary theory in the 1980s and 1990s has not focused on the difference between literary and nonliterary works. What theorists have done is to reflect on literature as a historical and ideological category, on the social and political functions that something called "literature" has been thought to perform. In nineteenth-century England, literature emerged as an extremely important idea, a special kind of writing charged with several functions. Made a subject of instruction in the colonies of the British Empire, it was charged with giving the natives an appreciation of the greatness of England and engaging them as grateful participants in a historic civilizing enterprise. At home it would counter the selfishness and materialism fostered by the new capitalist economy, offering the middle classes and the aristocrats alternative values and giving the workers a stake in the culture that, materially, relegated them to a subordinate position. It would at once teach disinterested appreciation, provide a sense of national greatness, create fellow-feeling among the classes, and ultimately, function as a replacement for religion, which seemed no longer to be able to hold society together.

Any set of texts that could do all that would be very special indeed. What is literature that it was thought to do all this? One thing that is crucial is a special structure of exemplarity at work in literature. A literary work—*Hamlet*, for instance—is characteristically the story of a fictional character: it presents itself as in some way exemplary (why else would you read it?), but it simultaneously declines to define the range or scope of that exemplarity—hence the ease with which readers and critics come to speak about the "universality" of literature. The structure of literary works is such that it is easier to take them as telling us about "the human condition" in general than to specify what narrower categories they describe or illuminate.

Is *Hamlet* just about princes, or men of the Renaissance, or introspective young men, or people whose fathers have died in obscure circumstances? Since all such answers seem unsatisfactory, it is easier for readers not to answer, thus implicitly accepting a possibility of universality. In their particularity, novels, poems, and plays decline to explore what they are exemplary *of* at the same time that they invite all readers to become involved in the predicaments and thoughts of their narrators and characters.

But the combination of offering universality and addressing all those who can read the language has had a powerful *national* function. Benedict Anderson argues, in *Imagined Communities: Reflections on the Origin and Spread of Nationalism,* a work of political history that has become influential as theory, that works of literature—particularly novels—helped to create national communities by their postulation of and appeal to a broad community of readers, bounded yet in principle open to all who could read the language. "Fiction," Anderson writes, "seeps quietly and continuously into reality, creating that remarkable confidence of community in anonymity which is the hallmark of modern nations." To present the characters, speakers, plots, and themes of English literature as potentially universal is to promote an open yet bounded imagined community to which subjects in the British colonies, for instance, are invited to aspire. In fact, the more the universality of literature is stressed, the more it may have a national function: asserting the universality of the vision of the world offered by Jane Austen makes England a very special place indeed, the site of standards of taste and behavior and, more important, of the moral scenarios and social circumstances in which ethical problems are worked out and personalities are formed.

Literature has been seen as a special kind of writing which, it was argued, could civilize not just the lower classes but also the aristocrats and the middle classes. This view of literature as an aesthetic object that could make us "better people" is linked to a certain idea of the subject, to what theorists have come to call "the liberal subject," the individual defined not by a social situation and interests but by an individual subjectivity (rationality and morality) conceived as essentially free of social determinants. The aesthetic object, cut off from practical purposes and inducing particular kinds of reflection and identifications, helps us to become liberal subjects through the free and disinterested exercise of an imaginative faculty that combines knowing and judging in the right relation. Literature does this, the argument goes, by encouraging consideration of complexities without a rush to judgment, engaging the mind in ethical issues, inducing readers to examine conduct (including their own) as an outsider or a reader of novels would. It promotes disinterestedness, teaches sensitivity and fine discriminations, produces identifications with men and women of other conditions, thus promoting fellow-feeling. In 1860 an educator maintained,

> by converse with the thoughts and utterances of those who are intellectual leaders of the race, our heart comes to beat in accord with the feeling of universal humanity. We discover that no differences of class, or party, or creed can destroy the power of genius to charm and to instruct, and that above the smoke and stir, the din and turmoil of man's lower life of care and business and debate, there is a serene and luminous region of truth where all may meet and expatiate in common.

Recent theoretical discussions have, not surprisingly, been critical of this conception of literature, and have focused above all on the mystification that seeks to distract workers from the misery of their condition by offering them access to this "higher region"—throwing the workers a few novels to keep them from throwing up a few barricades, as Terry Eagleton puts it. But when we explore claims about what literature does, how it works as a social practice, we find arguments that are exceedingly difficult to reconcile.

Literature has been given diametrically opposed functions. Is literature an ideological instrument: a set of stories that seduce readers into accepting the hierarchical arrangements of society? If stories take it for granted that women must find their happiness, if at all, in marriage; if they accept class divisions as natural and explore how the virtuous serving girl may marry a lord, they work to legitimate contingent historical arrangements. Or is literature the place where ideology is exposed, revealed as something that can be questioned? Literature represents, for example, in a potentially intense and affecting way, the narrow range of options historically offered to women, and, in making this visible, raises the possibility of *not* taking it for granted. Both claims are thoroughly plausible: that literature is the vehicle of ideology and that literature is an instrument for its undoing. Here again, we find a complex oscillation between potential "properties" of literature and attention that brings out these properties.

We also encounter contrary claims about the relation of literature to action. Theorists have maintained that literature encourages solitary reading and reflection as the way to engage with the world and thus counters the social and political activities that might produce change. At best it encourages detachment or appreciation of complexity, and at worst passivity and acceptance of what is. But on the other hand, literature has historically been seen as dangerous: it promotes the questioning of authority and social arrangements. Plato banned poets from his ideal republic because they could only do harm, and novels have long been credited with making people dissatisfied with the lives they inherit and eager for something new— whether life in big cities or romance or revolution. By promoting identification across divisions of class, gender, race, nation, and age, books may promote a "fellow-feeling" that discourages struggle; but they may also produce a keen sense of injustice that makes progressive struggles possible. Historically, works of literature are credited with producing change: Harriet Beecher Stowe's *Uncle Tom's Cabin*, a best seller in its day, helped create a revulsion against slavery that made possible the American Civil War.

I return in Chapter 7 to the problem of identification and its effects: what role does the identification with literary characters and narrators play? For the moment we should note above all the complexity and diversity of literature as an institution and social practice. What we have here, after all, is an institution based on the possibility of saying anything you can imagine. This is central to what literature is: for any orthodoxy, any belief, any value, a literary work can mock it, parody it, imagine some different and monstrous fiction. From the novels of the Marquis de Sade, which sought to work out what might happen in a world where action followed a nature conceived as unconstrained appetite, to Salman Rushdie's *The Satanic Verses*, which has caused so much outrage for its use of sacred names and motifs in a context of satire and parody, literature has been the possibility of fictionally exceeding what has previously been thought and written. For anything that seemed to make sense, literature could make it nonsense, go beyond it, transform it in a way that raised the question of its legitimacy and adequacy.

Literature has been the activity of a cultural elite, and it has been what is sometimes called "cultural capital": learning about literature gives you a stake in culture that may pay off in various ways, helping you fit

Theorists have assigned works of literature conflicting roles. They have been accused of lulling readers into detachment and even passivity in their reinforcement of established historical norms. However, they have also been blamed (or lauded) as being the spark that fires readers to initiate change. The philanthropist Harriet Beecher Stowe's *Uncle Tom's Cabin,* published in 1852, a scene from which is shown in an 1882 poster, is credited with creating a revulsion against slavery that helped make possible the American Civil War.

in with people of higher social status. But literature cannot be reduced to this conservative social function: it is scarcely the purveyor of "family values" but makes seductive all manner of crimes, from Satan's revolt against God in Milton's *Paradise Lost* to Raskolnikov's murder of an old woman in Dostoyevsky's *Crime and Punishment*. It encourages resistance to capitalist values, to the practicalities of getting and spending. Literature is the noise of culture as well as its information. It is an entropic force as well as cultural capital. It is a writing that calls for a reading and engages readers in problems of meaning.

The Paradox of Literature

Literature is a paradoxical institution because to create literature is to write according to existing formulas—to produce something that looks like a sonnet or that follows the conventions of the novel—but it is also to flout those conventions, to go beyond them. Literature is an institution that lives by exposing and criticizing its own limits, by testing what will happen if one writes differently. So literature is at the same time the name for the utterly conventional—*moon* rhymes with *June* and *swoon*, maidens are fair, knights are bold—and for the utterly disruptive, where readers have to struggle to create any meaning at all, as in sentences like this from James Joyce's *Finnegans Wake*: "Eins within a space and a wearywide space it was er wohned a Mookse."

The question "What is literature?" arises, I suggested earlier, not because people are worried that they might mistake a novel for history or the message in a fortune cookie for a poem but because critics and theorists hope, by saying what literature is, to promote what they take to be the most pertinent critical methods and to dismiss methods that neglect the most basic and distinctive aspects of literature. In the context of recent theory, the question "What is literature?" matters because theory has highlighted the literariness of texts of all sorts. To reflect on literariness is to keep before us, as resources for analyzing these discourses, reading practices elicited by literature: the suspension of the demand for immediate intelligibility, reflection on the implications of means of expression, and attention to how meaning is made and pleasure produced.

TEN CEN[T]

THRILLING

Love

10¢ Dec.

Beginning
FORGOTTEN [G]
By MARCELLE LAT[HAM]

Stories
by
Popular
Authors

FEATURING
ALL-AMERICAN
LOVE
A Complete
Book-Length Novel
By HELEN AHERN

THREE

Literature and Cultural Studies

●

PROFESSORS OF FRENCH WRITING BOOKS about cigarettes or Americans' obsession with fat; Shakespearians analyzing bisexuality; experts on realism working on serial killers. What is going on?

What's happening here is "cultural studies," a major activity in the humanities in the 1990s. Some literature professors may have turned away from Milton to Madonna, from Shakespeare to soap operas, abandoning the study of literature altogether. How does this relate to literary theory?

Theory has enormously enriched and invigorated the study of literary works, but as I noted in Chapter 1, theory is not the theory *of literature*. If you had to say what "theory" is the theory *of,* the answer would be something like "signifying practices," the production and representation of experience, and the constitution of human subjects—in short, something like

Popular culture is increasingly an object of critical theorizing and analysis. *Thrilling Love—Stories by Popular Authors,* with a football player and a woman in a fur coat embracing and smiling at each other, was published in 1933.

culture in the broadest sense. And it is striking that the field of cultural studies, as it has developed, is as confusingly interdisciplinary and as difficult to define as "theory" itself. One could say that the two go together: "theory" is the theory and cultural studies the practice. *Cultural studies is the practice of which what we call "theory" for short is the theory.* Some practitioners of cultural studies complain about "high theory," but this indicates an understandable desire not to be held responsible for the endless and intimidating corpus of theory. Work in cultural studies is, in fact, deeply

What does it mean for the literary canon when scholars study twentieth-century pop culture figures, such as Madonna, as well as the brilliant seventeenth-century English poet John Milton (shown dictating to one of his daughters in a Delacroix painting from about 1826).

dependent on the theoretical debates about meaning, identity, representation, and agency that I take up in this book.

But what is the relation between literary studies and cultural studies? In its broadest conception, the project of cultural studies is to understand the functioning of culture, particularly in the modern world: how cultural productions work and how cultural identities are constructed and organized, for individuals and groups, in a world of diverse and intermingled communities, state power, media industries, and multinational corporations. In principle, then, cultural studies includes and encompasses literary studies, examining literature as a particular cultural practice. But what kind of inclusion is this? There's a good deal of argument here. Is cultural studies a capacious project within which literary studies gains new power and insight? Or will cultural studies swallow up literary studies and destroy literature? To grasp the problem we need a bit of background about the development of cultural studies.

The Emergence of Cultural Studies

Modern cultural studies has a double ancestry. It comes first from French structuralism of the 1960s (see Appendix), which treated culture (including literature) as a series of practices whose rules or conventions should be described. An early work of cultural studies by the French literary theorist Roland Barthes, *Mythologies* (1957), undertakes brief "readings" of a range of cultural activities, from professional wrestling and the advertising of cars and detergents to such mythical cultural objects as French wine and Einstein's brain. Barthes is especially interested in demystifying what in culture comes to seem natural by showing that it is based on contingent, historical constructions. In analyzing cultural practices, he identifies the underlying conventions and their social implications. If you compare professional wrestling with boxing, for instance, you can see that there are different conventions: boxers behave stoically when hit, while wrestlers writhe in agony and flamboyantly enact stereotyped roles. In boxing the rules of the contest are external to the match, in the sense that they designate limits beyond which it must not go, while in wrestling the rules are very much *within* the match, as conventions that increase the range of meaning that can be produced: rules exist to be violated, quite flagrantly, so that the "bad guy" or villain may dramatically reveal himself as evil and unsporting and the audience be whipped up into vengeful fury. Wrestling thus provides above all the satisfactions of moral intelligibility, as good and evil are clearly opposed. Investigating cultural practices from high literature to fashion and food, Barthes's example encouraged the reading of the connotations

Professional wrestling offers the satisfaction of moral intelligibility, clearly demarcating good and evil. This image shows pro wrestlers Triple H and Batista in a 2005 WrestleMania bout.

of cultural images and analysis of the social functioning of the strange constructions of culture.

The other source of contemporary cultural studies is Marxist literary theory in Britain. The work of Raymond Williams (*Culture and Society*, 1958) and of the founder of the Birmingham Centre for Contemporary Cultural Studies, Richard Hoggart (*The Uses of Literacy*, 1957), sought to recover and explore a popular, working-class culture that had been lost sight of as culture was identified with high literature. This project of recovering lost voices, of doing history from below, encountered another theorization of culture—from European Marxist theory—which analyzed mass culture (as opposed to "popular culture") as an oppressive ideological formation, as meanings functioning to position readers or viewers as consumers and to justify the workings of state power. The interaction between these two analyses of culture—culture as an expression *of* the people and culture as imposition *on* the people—has been crucial to the development of cultural studies, first in Britain and then elsewhere.

Tensions

Cultural studies in this tradition is driven by the tension between the desire to recover popular culture as the expression of the people or give voice to the culture of marginalized groups, and the study of mass culture as an ideological imposition, an oppressive ideological formation. On the one hand, the point of studying popular culture is to get in touch with what is important for the lives of ordinary people—their culture—as opposed to that of aesthetes and professors. On the other, there is a strong impetus to show how people are shaped or manipulated by cultural forces. How far are people constructed as subjects by cultural forms and practices, which "interpellate" or address them *as* people with particular desires and values?

The concept of *interpellation* comes from the French Marxist theorist Louis Althusser. You are addressed—by ads, for instance—as a particular sort of subject (a consumer who values certain qualities), and by being repeatedly hailed in this way you come to occupy such a position. Cultural studies asks how far we are manipulated by cultural forms and how far or in what ways we are able to use them for other purposes, exercising "agency," as it is called. (The question of "agency," to use the shorthand of current theory, is the question of how far we can be subjects responsible for our actions and how far our apparent choices are constrained by forces we do not control.)

Cultural studies dwells in the tension between the analyst's desire to analyze culture as a set of codes and practices that alienates people from their interests and creates the desires that they come to have and, on the other hand, the analyst's wish to find in popular culture an authentic expression of value. One solution is to show that people are able to use the cultural materials foisted upon them by capitalism and its media industries to make a culture of their own. Popular culture is made from mass

James Montgomery Flagg's iconic Uncle Sam poster is an example of interpellation, wherein the reader or viewer is addressed as a particular sort of person; after repeatedly being referred to in this way, the reader takes on this assigned role.

Algerian-born French Marxist philosopher Louis Althusser was widely influential: Both Foucault and Derrida studied under him, and Judith Butler has adapted and revised Althusser's concept of interpellation. A lifelong member of the French Communist Party, he is shown in this 1978 photo reading the organization's newspaper, *L'Humanité.*

culture. Popular culture is made from cultural resources that are opposed to it and thus is a culture of struggle, a culture whose creativity consists in using the products of mass culture.

Work in cultural studies has been particularly attuned to the problematical character of identity and to the multiple ways in which identities are formed, experienced, and transmitted. Particularly important, therefore, has been the study of the unstable cultures and cultural identities that arise for groups—ethnic minorities, immigrants, women—that may have trouble identifying with the larger culture in which they find themselves—a culture which is itself a shifting ideological construction.

Now the relationship between cultural studies and literary studies is a complicated problem. In theory, cultural studies is all-encompassing:

Shakespeare and rap music, high culture and low, culture of the past and culture of the present. But in practice, since meaning is based on difference, people do cultural studies *as opposed* to something else. As opposed to what? Since cultural studies arose out of literary studies, the answer often is, "as opposed to literary studies, traditionally conceived," where the task was the interpretation of literary works as the achievements of their authors, and the main justification for studying literature was the special value of great works: their complexity, their beauty, their insight, their universality, and their potential benefits to the reader.

But literary studies itself has never been unified around a single conception of what it was doing, traditional or otherwise; and since the advent of theory, literary studies has been an especially contentious and contested discipline, where all kinds of projects, treating both literary and nonliterary works, compete for attention.

In principle, then, there need not be conflict between literary and cultural studies. Literary studies is not committed to a conception of the literary object that cultural studies must repudiate. Cultural studies arose as the application of techniques of literary analysis to other cultural materials. It treats cultural artifacts as "texts" to be read rather than as objects that are simply there to be counted. And, conversely, literary studies may gain when literature is studied as a particular cultural practice and works are related to other discourses. The impact of theory has been to expand the range of questions to which literary works can answer and to focus attention on the different ways they resist or complicate the ideas of their age. In principle, cultural studies, with its insistence on studying literature as one signifying practice among others, and on examining the culture roles with which literature has been invested, can intensify the study of literature as a complex intertextual phenomenon.

Arguments about the relation between literary and cultural studies can be grouped around two broad topics: (1) what is called the "literary canon": the works regularly studied in schools and universities and deemed to form "our literary heritage"; (2) the appropriate methods for analyzing cultural objects.

1. The Literary Canon

What will become of the literary canon if cultural studies swallows literary studies? Have the soaps replaced Shakespeare and, if so, is cultural studies to blame? Won't cultural studies kill literature by encouraging the study of films, television, and other popular cultural forms rather than the classics of world literature?

A similar charge was made against theory when it encouraged the reading of philosophical and psychoanalytic texts along with literary works: it took students away from the classics. But theory has reinvigorated the traditional literary canon, opening the door to more ways of reading the "great works" of English and American literature. Never has so much been written about Shakespeare; he is studied from every angle conceivable, interpreted in feminist, Marxist, psychoanalytic, historicist, and deconstructive vocabularies. Wordsworth has been transformed by literary theory from a poet of nature to a key figure of modernity. What *have* suffered neglect are "minor" works that were regularly studied when literary study was organized to "cover" historical periods and genres. Shakespeare is more widely read and vigorously interpreted than ever, but Marlowe, Beaumont and Fletcher, Dekker, Heywood, and Ben Jonson—Elizabethan and Jacobean dramatists who used to surround him—are little read today.

Would cultural studies have a similar effect, providing new contexts and increasing the range of issues for a few literary works, while taking

Shakespeare is still studied today from every possible perspective, but many of the works of the dramatists who surrounded him, including Ben Jonson and Christopher Marlowe, are ignored. Shown are a poster for a Federal Theatre Project presentation of Jonson's *Volpone* at the Mayan Theatre (between 1936 and 1941), a facsimile of a poster for a Federal Theatre Project presentation of *Faustus* at Maxine Elliott's Theatre (between 1930 and 1950), and a scene from a 2003 production of Shakespeare's *A Winter's Tale* at Théâtre de la Tempête in Paris.

students away from others? So far, the growth of cultural studies has accompanied (though not caused) an expansion of the literary canon. Literature that is widely taught today includes writings by women and members of other historically marginalized groups. Whether added to traditional literary courses or studied as separate traditions ("Asian American literature," "post-colonial literature in English"), these writings are often studied as representations of the experience and thus culture of the people in question (in the United States, of African Americans, Asian Americans, Native Americans, and US Latinos, as well as women). Such writings, though, bring to the fore questions about how far literature creates the culture it is said to express or represent. Is culture the *effect* of representations rather than their source or cause?

The widespread study of previously neglected writings has prompted heated arguments in the media: have traditional literary standards been compromised? Are previously neglected works selected for their "literary excellence" or their cultural representativeness? Is it "political correctness," the desire to give every minority just representation, rather than specifically literary criteria, that is determining the choice of works to be studied?

There are three lines of response to such questions. The first is that "literary excellence" has never determined what is studied. Each teacher does not pick what he or she thinks are the ten greatest works of world literature but, rather, selects works that are representative of something: perhaps a literary form or a period of literary history (the English novel, Elizabethan literature, modern American poetry). It is within that context of representing something that the "best" works are chosen: you don't omit Sidney, Spenser, and Shakespeare from your Elizabethan course if you think they are the best poets of the period, just as you include what you take to be the "best" works of Asian American literature, if that is what you are teaching. What

Sixteenth-century soldier, poet, and courtier Sir Philip Sidney completed his *Defence of Poesie* when he was just twenty-six years old. Knighted in 1583 and appointed governor of Flushing in the Netherlands in 1585 by Elizabeth I, he was wounded in the Battle of Zutphen in 1586. He died less than a month later at the age of thirty-one and was memorialized by his contemporary and the Tudor poet laureate Edmund Spenser in *Astrophel*.

has changed is an interest in choosing works to represent a range of cultural experiences as well as a range of literary forms.

Second, application of the criterion of literary excellence has historically been compromised by nonliterary criteria involving race and gender, for instance. A boy's experience of growing up (e.g., Huck Finn's) has been deemed universal, whereas a girl's (Maggie Tulliver's in *The Mill on the Floss*) has been seen as a subject of more restricted interest.

Finally, the notion of literary excellence itself has been subjected to debate: does it enshrine particular cultural interests and purposes as if they were the only standard of literary evaluation? Debate about what has counted as literature worthy of study and how ideas of excellence have functioned in institutions is a strand of cultural studies extremely pertinent to literary studies.

2. Modes of Analysis

The second broad topic of dissension concerns the modes of analysis in literary and cultural studies. When cultural studies was a renegade form of literary studies, it applied literary analysis to other cultural materials. If cultural studies became dominant and its practitioners no longer came to it from literary studies, might not that application of literary analysis become less important? The introduction to an influential American volume, *Cultural Studies,* declares, "although there is no prohibition against close textual readings in cultural studies, they are also not required." This assurance that close reading is not prohibited is scarcely reassuring to the literary critic. Freed from the principle that has long governed literary studies—that the main point of interest is the distinctive complexity of individual works—cultural studies could easily become a kind of nonquantitative sociology, treating works as instances or symptoms of something else rather than of interest in themselves, and succumbing to other temptations.

Chief among these is the lure of "totality," the notion that there is a social totality of which cultural forms are the expression or the symptom, so that to analyze them is to relate them to the social totality from which they derive. Recent theory debates the question of whether there is a social totality, a sociopolitical configuration, and if so, how cultural products and activities relate to it. But cultural studies is drawn to the idea of a direct relationship, in which cultural products are the symptom of an underlying sociopolitical configuration. For example, the "Popular Culture" course of the Open University in Britain, which was taken by some five thousand people between 1982 and 1985, contained a unit on "Television Police Series and Law and Order," which analyzed the development of police series in terms of a changing sociopolitical situation.

"Dixon of Dock Green" centres on a paternalistic father-figure who is intimately familiar with the working class neighbourhood he patrols. With the consolidation of the welfare state in the prosperity of the early 1960s, class problems become translated into social concerns: corresponding to this, a new series, "Z Cars," shows uniformed police in patrol cars doing their job as professionals but at some distance from the community they serve. After the 1960s there is a crisis for hegemony[1] in Britain, and the state, unable to win consent easily, needs to arm itself against opposition from trade union militancy, "terrorists," the IRA. This more aggressively mobilized state of hegemony is reflected in such examples of the police genre as "The Sweeney" and "The Professionals" in which plain-clothes cops

---

[1] *Hegemony* is an arrangement of domination accepted by those who are dominated. Ruling groups dominate not by pure force but through a structure of consent, and culture is part of this structure that legitimizes current social arrangements. (The concept comes from the Italian Marxist theorist Antonio Gramsci.)

typically combat a terrorist organization by matching its violence with their own.

This is certainly interesting and may well be true, which makes it all the more alluring as a mode of analysis, but it involves a shift from reading ("close reading") that is alert to the details of narrative structure and attends to complexities of meaning, to a sociopolitical analysis, in which all the serials of a given era have the same significance, as expressions of the social configuration. If literary studies is subsumed into cultural studies, this sort of "symptomatic interpretation" might become the norm; the specificity of cultural objects might be neglected, along with the reading practices which literature invites (discussed in Chapter 2). The suspension of the demand for immediate intelligibility, the willingness to work at the boundaries of meaning, opening oneself to unexpected, productive effects of language and imagination, and the interest in how meaning and pleasure are produced—these dispositions are particularly valuable, not just for reading literature but also for considering other cultural phenomena, though it is literary study that makes these reading practices available.

Goals

Finally there is the question of the goals of literary and cultural studies. Practitioners of cultural studies often hope that work on present culture will be an intervention in culture rather than mere description. "Cultural studies thus believes," the editors of *Cultural Studies* conclude, "that its own intellectual work is supposed to—can—make a difference." This is an odd statement but, I think, a revealing one: cultural studies does not believe that its intellectual work *will* make a difference. That would be overweening, not to say naive. It believes that its work "is supposed to" make a difference. That is the idea.

Historically, the ideas of studying popular culture and of making one's work a political intervention are closely linked. In Britain in the 1960s and 1970s studying working-class culture had a political charge. In Britain, where national cultural identity seemed linked to monuments of high culture—Shakespeare and the tradition of English literature, for example—the very fact of studying popular culture was an act of resistance, in a way that it isn't in the United States, where national identity has often been defined *against* high culture. Mark Twain's *Huckleberry Finn*, the work which does as much as any other to define Americanness, ends with Huck Finn lighting out for "the territories" because Aunt Sally wants to "sivilize" him. His identity depends on escaping civilized culture. Traditionally the American is the man on the run from culture.

The boy's experience of growing up—Mark Twain's hero Huck Finn—is considered representative of the universal experience of growing up, whereas the girl's experience—George Eliot's Maggie Tolliver, for example—is seen as a special case, revealing a gender-based fault in the designation of the label of literary excellence. The very definition of Americanness, *Huckleberry Finn* turns on Huck's desire to break free of the defined culture or civilization to which his aunt Sally wants him to belong.

When cultural studies denigrates literature as elitist, this is hard to distinguish from a long national tradition of bourgeois philistinism. In the United States shunning high culture and studying popular culture is not a politically radical or resistant gesture so much as a rendering academic of mass culture. Cultural studies in America has few of the links with political movements that have energized cultural studies in Britain, and it could be seen as primarily a resourceful, interdisciplinary, but still academic study of cultural practices and cultural representation. Cultural studies is "supposed to be" radical, but the opposition between an activist cultural studies and a passive literary studies may be wishful thinking.

Distinctions

Debates about the relation between literature and cultural studies are replete with complaints about elitism and charges that studying popular culture will bring the death of literature. In all the confusion, it helps to separate two sets of questions. The first are questions about the value of studying one sort of cultural object or another. The value of studying Shakespeare rather than soap operas can no longer be taken for granted and needs to be argued: what can different sorts of studies achieve, in the way of intellectual and moral training, for example? Such arguments are not easy to make: the example of German concentration camp commanders who were connoisseurs of literature, art, and music has complicated attempts to make claims for the effects of particular sorts of study. But these issues should be confronted head-on.

A different set of questions involves the *methods* for the study of cultural objects of all sorts—the advantages and disadvantages of different modes of interpretation and analysis, such as interpreting cultural objects as complex structures or reading them as symptoms of social totalities.

Though appreciative interpretation has been associated with literary studies and symptomatic analysis with cultural studies, either mode can go with either sort of cultural object. Close reading of nonliterary writing does not imply aesthetic valuation of the object, any more than asking cultural questions of literary works implies that they are just documents of a period. In the next chapter I pursue further the problem of interpretation.

THE ENCHANTED WOODS

FOUR

Language, Meaning, and Interpretation

⬤

IS LITERATURE A SPECIAL KIND OF LANGUAGE or is it a special use of language? Is it language organized in distinctive ways or is it language granted special privileges? I argued in Chapter 2 that it won't work to choose one option or the other: literature involves *both* properties of language *and* a special kind of attention to language. As this debate indicates, questions about the nature and the roles of language and how to analyze it have been central to theory. Some of the major issues can be focused through the problem of meaning. What is involved in thinking about meaning?

Literature involves *both* properties of language and a special kind of attention to language. Some of the major issues that arise in a discussion of the language of literature derive from the different levels and varieties of meaning at play—for example, in Robert Frost's two-line poem "The Secret Sits," the meaning of the act of uttering these words in particular circumstances, the meaning of the poem as a whole, and the meaning of a word in that text, *dance*, for example, in "We dance round in a ring and suppose," the poem's first line. *The Enchanted Woods* by H. Thomas Maybank shows three girls dancing in a circle in the woods. It was created in 1914.

Meaning in Literature

Take the lines which we earlier treated as literature, a two-line poem by Robert Frost:

> **The Secret Sits**
> *We dance round in a ring and suppose,*
> *But the Secret sits in the middle and knows.*

What is "meaning" here? Well, there's a difference between asking about the meaning of a text (the poem as a whole) and the meaning of a word. We can say that *dance* means "to perform a succession of rhythmic and patterned movements," but what does this text mean? It suggests, you might say, the futility of human doings: we go around and around; we can only suppose. More than that, with its rhyme and its air of knowing what it is doing, this text engages the reader in a process of puzzling over dancing and supposing. That effect, the process the text can provoke, is part of its meaning. So, we have the meaning of a word and the meaning or provocations of a text; then, in between, there's what we might call the meaning of an utterance: the meaning of the act of uttering these words in particular circumstances. What *act* is this utterance performing: is it *warning* or *admitting*, *lamenting* or *boasting*, for example? Who is "we" here and what does "dancing" mean in this utterance?

We can't just ask about "meaning," then. There are at least three different dimensions or levels of meaning: the meaning of a word, of an utterance, and of a text. Possible meanings of words contribute to the meaning of an utterance, which is an act by a speaker. (And the meanings of words, in turn, come from the things they might do in utterances.) Finally, the text, which here represents an unknown speaker making this enigmatical utterance, is something an author has constructed, and its meaning is not a proposition but what it *does*, its potential to affect readers.

We have different kinds of meaning, but one thing we can say in general is that meaning is based on difference. We don't know who "we" refers to in this text; only that it is "we" as opposed to "I" alone, and to "he," "she," "it," "you," and "they." "We" is some indefinite plural group that includes whatever speaker we think is involved. Is the reader included in "we" or not? Is "we" everyone except the Secret, or is it a special group? Such questions, which have no easy answers, come up in any attempt to interpret the poem. What we have are contrasts, differences.

Much the same could be said of "dance" and "suppose." What "dance" means here depends on what we contrast it with ("dancing around" as opposed to "proceeding directly" or as opposed to "remaining still"); and "suppose" is opposed to "know." Thinking about the meaning of this poem is a matter of working with oppositions or differences, giving them content, extrapolating from them.

Saussure's Theory of Language

A language is a *system* of differences. So declares Ferdinand de Saussure, a Swiss linguist of the early twentieth century whose work has been crucial to contemporary theory. What makes each element of a language what it is, what gives it its identity, are the contrasts between it and other elements within the system of the language. Saussure offers an analogy: a train—say the 8:30 a.m. London-to-Oxford express—depends for its identity on the system of trains, as described in the railway timetable. So the 8:30 London-to-Oxford express is distinguished from the 9:30 London-to-Cambridge express and the 8:45 Oxford local. What counts are not any of the physical features of a particular train: the engine, the carriages, the exact route, the personnel, and so on may all vary, as may the times of departure and arrival; the train may leave and arrive late. What gives the train its identity is its place in the system of trains: it is this train, *as opposed to* the others. As Saussure says of the linguistic sign, "Its most precise characteristic is to be what the others are not." Similarly, the letter *b* may be written in any number of different ways (think of different people's handwriting), so long as it is not confused with other letters, such as *l, k,* and *d*. What is crucial is not any particular form or content, but differences, which enable it to signify.

For Saussure, a language is a system of signs and the key fact is what he calls the arbitrary nature of the linguistic sign. This means two things. First, the sign (for instance, a word) is a combination of a form (the "signifier") and a meaning (the "signified"), and the relation between form and meaning is based on convention, not natural resemblance. What I am sitting on is called a *chair* but could perfectly well have been called something else—*wab* or *punce*. It's a convention or rule of English that

The Swiss linguist Ferdinand de Saussure (1857–1913) wrote only one full-length work, *Thesis on the Primitive Vowel System in Indo-European Languages,* when he was twenty-one. Saussure was a critically influential teacher, however, lecturing in Paris and at the University of Geneva for decades; his *Course in General Linguistics* was constructed from his lecture notes by colleagues after his death. Saussure proposed that what gives each element of a language its identity is its differences from all the other elements in that system of language.

it is the one rather than the other; in other languages it would have quite different names. The cases we think of as exceptions are "onomatopoeic" words, where the sound seems to imitate what it represents, like *bow-wow*, or *buzz*. But these differ from one language to another: in French dogs say "oua-oua" and *buzz* is *bourdonner*.

Even more important, for Saussure and recent theory, is the second aspect of the arbitrary nature of the sign: both the signifier (form) and the signified (meaning) are themselves conventional divisions of the plane of sound and the plane of thought, respectively. Languages divide up the plane of sound and the plane of thought differently. English distinguishes *chair, cheer*, and *char* on the plane of sound, as separate signs with different meanings, but it need not do so—these could be variant pronunciations of a single sign. On the plane of meaning, English distinguishes *chair* from *stool* (a chair without a back) but allows the signified or concept *chair* to include seats with and without arms, and both hard seats and soft luxurious seats—two differences that could perfectly well involve distinct concepts.

A language, Saussure insists, is not a "nomenclature" that provides its own names for categories that exist outside language. This is a point with crucial ramifications for recent theory. We tend to assume that we have the words *dog* and *chair* in order to name dogs and chairs, which exist outside any language. But, Saussure argues, if words stood for preexisting concepts, they would have exact equivalents in meaning from one language to the next, which is not at all the case. Each language is a system of concepts as well as forms: a system of conventional signs that organizes the world.

Language and Thought

How language relates to thought has been a major issue for recent theory. At one extreme is the commonsense view that language just provides names for thoughts that exist independently; language offers ways of expressing preexisting thoughts. At the other extreme is the "Sapir-Whorf hypothesis," named after two linguists who claimed that the language we speak determines what we can think. For instance, Whorf argued that the Hopi Indians have a conception of time that can't be grasped in English (and so can't be explained here!). There seems no way of demonstrating that there are thoughts of one language that can't be thought or expressed in another, but we do have massive evidence that one language makes "natural" or "normal" thoughts that require a special effort in another.

The linguistic code is a theory of the world. Different languages divide up the world differently. Speakers of English have "pets"—a category to

The Sapir-Whorf hypothesis is named after American linguist Edward Sapir and his student Benjamin Lee Whorf. Sapir and Whorf claimed that the language we speak determines what we can think. Whorf maintained, for example, that the Hopi Indians, who are known for their agricultural skills as well as intricate pottery, have a conception of time that cannot be expressed in the English language. In this image from around 1900, a Hopi woman decorates a ceramic vessel.

Nineteenth-century French poet Paul Verlaine plays on grammatical structure in his poem "Il pleure dans mon coeur," published in Verlaine's *Romances sans paroles* in 1891. The poet is shown in a painting by French artist Gustave Courbet.

which nothing in French corresponds, though the French possess inordinate numbers of dogs and cats. English compels us to learn the sex of an infant so as to use the correct pronoun to talk about him or her (you can't call a baby "it"); our language thus implies that the sex is crucial (whence, no doubt, the popularity of pink or blue garments, to signal the right answer to speakers). But this linguistic marking of sex is in no way inevitable; all languages don't make sex the crucial feature of newborns. Grammatical structures, too, are conventions of a language, not natural or inevitable. When we look up in the sky and see a movement of wings, our language could perfectly well have us say something like "It's winging" (as we say, "It's raining"), rather than "Birds are flying." A famous poem by Paul Verlaine plays on this structure: "Il pleure dans mon coeur / Comme il pleut sur la ville" (It cries in my heart

/ As it rains on the town). We say "it's raining in town"; why not "it's crying in my heart"?

Language is not a "nomenclature" that provides labels for preexisting categories; it generates its own categories. But speakers and readers can be brought to see through and around the settings of their language, so as to see a different reality. Works of literature explore the settings or categories of habitual ways of thinking and frequently attempt to bend or reshape them, showing us how to think something that our language had not previously anticipated, forcing us to attend to the categories through which we unthinkingly view the world. Language is thus both the concrete manifestation of ideology—the categories in which speakers are authorized to think—and the site of its questioning or undoing.

Linguistic Analysis

Saussure distinguishes the system of a language (*la langue*) from particular instances of speech and writing (*parole*). The task of linguistics is to reconstruct the underlying system (or grammar) of a language that makes possible the speech events or *parole*. This involves a further distinction between *synchronic* study of a language (focusing on a language as a system at a particular time, present or past) and *diachronic* study, which looks at the historical changes to particular elements of the language. To understand a language as a functioning system is to look at it synchronically, trying to spell out the rules and conventions of the system that make possible the forms and meanings of the language. The most influential linguist of our day, Noam Chomsky, the founder of what is called transformational-generative grammar, goes further, arguing that the task of linguistics is to reconstruct the "linguistic competence" of native speakers: the implicit knowledge or ability speakers acquire and

American linguist Noam Chomsky, known as the father of modern linguistics, is also an outspoken critic of US foreign policy. A professor at the Massachusetts Institute of Technology, he travels widely to speak on politics. He is shown here in a 2002 photo in his office at MIT.

which enables them to speak and to understand even sentences they have never before encountered.

So linguistics *starts* from facts about the form and meaning utterances have for speakers and tries to account for them. How is it that the following two sentences with similar forms—*John is eager to please* and *John is easy to please*—have rather different meanings for speakers of English? Speakers know that in the first John wants to please and that in the second others do the pleasing. A linguist does not try to discover the "true meaning" of these sentences, as if people had been wrong all along and deep down the sentences mean something else. The task of linguistics is to describe the structures of English (here, by positing an underlying level of grammatical structure) so as to account for attested differences in meaning between these sentences.

Poetics Versus Hermeneutics

Here there is a basic distinction, too often neglected in literary studies, between two kinds of projects: one, modeled on linguistics, takes meanings as what have to be accounted for and tries to work out how they are possible. The other, by contrast, starts with forms and seeks to interpret them, to tell us what they really mean. In literary studies, this is a contrast between *poetics* and *hermeneutics*. Poetics starts with attested meanings or effects and asks how they are achieved. (What makes this passage in a novel seem ironic? What makes us sympathize with this particular character? Why is the ending of this poem ambiguous?) Hermeneutics, on the other hand, starts with texts and asks what they mean, seeking to discover new and better interpretations. Hermeneutic models come from the fields of law and religion, where people seek to interpret an authoritative legal or sacred text in order to decide how to act.

The linguistic model suggests that literary study should take the first track, of poetics, trying to understand how works achieve the effects they do, but the modern tradition of criticism has overwhelmingly taken the second, making the interpretation of individual works the payoff of literary study. In fact, works of literary criticism often combine poetics and hermeneutics, asking how a particular effect is achieved or why an ending seems right (both matters of poetics), but also asking what a particular line means and what a poem tells us about the human condition (hermeneutics). But the two projects are in principle quite distinct, with different goals and different kinds of evidence. Taking meanings or effects as the point of departure (poetics) is fundamentally different from seeking to discover meaning (hermeneutics).

If literary studies took linguistics as a model, its task would be to describe the "literary competence" that readers of literature acquire. A poetics describing literary competence would focus on the conventions that make possible literary structure and meaning: what are the codes or systems of convention that enable readers to identify literary genres, recognize plots, create "characters" out of the scattered details provided in the text, identify themes in literary works, and pursue the kind of symbolic interpretation that allows us to gauge the significance of poems and stories?

This analogy between poetics and linguistics may seem misleading, for we don't know the meaning of a literary work as we know the meaning of *John is eager to please* and therefore can't take meaning as a given but have to seek it. This is certainly one reason why literary studies in modern times have favored hermeneutics over poetics (the other reason is that people generally study literary works not because they are interested in the functioning of literature but because they think these works have important things to tell them and want to know what they are). But poetics does not require that we know the meaning of a work; its task is to account for whatever effects we can attest to—for example, that one ending is more successful than another, that this combination of images in a poem makes sense while another does not. Moreover, a crucial part of poetics is an account of how readers do go about interpreting literary works—what are the conventions that enable them to make sense of works as they do. For instance, what I called in Chapter 2 the "hyper-protected cooperative principle" is a basic convention that makes possible the interpretation of literature: the assumption that difficulties, apparent nonsense, digressions, and irrelevancies have a relevant function at some level.

Readers and Meaning

The idea of literary competence focuses attention on the implicit knowledge that readers (and writers) bring to their encounters with texts: what sort of procedures do readers follow in responding to works as they do? What sort of assumptions must be in place to account for their reactions and interpretations? Thinking about readers and the way they make sense of literature has led to what has been called "reader-response criticism," which claims that the meaning of the text is the experience of the reader (an experience that includes hesitations, conjectures, and self-corrections). If a literary work is conceived as a succession of actions upon the understanding of a reader, then an interpretation of the work can be a story of that encounter, with its ups and downs: various conventions or expectations are brought into play, connections are posited, and expectations defeated or confirmed. To interpret a work is to tell a story of reading.

But the story one can tell about a given work depends upon what theorists have called the reader's "horizon of expectations." A work is interpreted as answering questions posed by this horizon of expectations, and a reader of the 1990s approaches *Hamlet* with expectations different from those of a contemporary of Shakespeare's. A whole range of factors can affect readers' horizons of expectations. Feminist criticism has debated what difference it makes, what difference it should make, if the reader is a woman. How, Elaine Showalter asks, does "the hypothesis of a female reader change our apprehension of a given text, awakening us to the significance of its sexual codes?" Literary texts and the traditions of their interpretation seem to have presumed a male reader and induced women readers to read as a man, from a male point of view. Similarly, film theorists have hypothesized that what they call the cinematic gaze (the view from the position of the camera) is essentially male: women are positioned as the object of the cinematic gaze rather than as the observer. In literary studies feminist critics have studied the various strategies by which works make a male perspective the normative one and have debated how the study of such structures and effects should change ways of reading—for men as well as women.

Interpretation

Focus on historical and social variations in ways of reading emphasizes that interpreting is a social practice. Readers interpret informally when they talk to friends about books or films; they interpret to themselves as they read. For the more formal interpretation that takes place in classrooms, there are different protocols. For any element of a work, you can ask what it does, how it relates to other elements, but interpretation may ultimately involve playing the "about" game: "So, what is this work really about?" This question is not prompted by the obscurity of a text; it is even more appropriate for simple texts than for wickedly complex ones. In this game the answer must meet certain conditions: it cannot be obvious, for instance; it must be speculative. To say "*Hamlet* is about a prince in Denmark" is to refuse to play the game. But "*Hamlet* is about the breakdown of the Elizabethan world order," or "*Hamlet* is about men's fear of feminine sexuality," or "*Hamlet* is about the unreliability of signs" count as possible answers. What are commonly seen as "schools" of literary criticism or theoretical "approaches" to literature are, from the point of view of hermeneutics, dispositions to give particular kinds of answers to the question of what a work is ultimately "about": "the class struggle" (Marxism), "the possibility of unifying experience" (the New Criticism), "Oedipal conflict" (psychoanalysis), "the containment of subversive energies" (new historicism), "the asymmetry of gender relations" (feminism), "the self-deconstructive nature of the text" (deconstruction), "the occlusion of imperialism" (post-colonial theory), "the heterosexual matrix" (gay and lesbian studies).

The theoretical discourses named in parentheses are not primarily modes of interpretation: they are accounts of what they take to be particularly

important to culture and society. Many of these theories include accounts of the functioning of literature or of discourse generally, and so partake of the project of poetics; but as versions of hermeneutics they give rise to particular types of interpretation in which texts are mapped into a target language. What is important in the game of interpretation is not the answer you come up with—as my parodies show, some versions of the answer become, by definition, predictable. What's important is how you get there, what you do with the details of the text in relating them to your answer.

But how do we choose between interpretations? As my examples may suggest, at one level there is no need to decide whether *Hamlet* is "ultimately about," say, Renaissance politics, men's relations to their mothers, or the unreliability of signs. The liveliness of the institution of literary study depends on the twin facts that (1) such arguments are never settled, and (2) arguments have to be made about how particular scenes or combinations of lines support any particular hypothesis. You can't make a work mean just anything: it resists, and you have to labor to convince others of the pertinence of your reading. For the conduct of such arguments, a key question is what determines meaning. We return to this central issue.

Meaning, Intention, and Context

What determines meaning? Sometimes we say that the meaning of an utterance is what someone means by it, as though the intention of a speaker determined meaning. Sometimes we say meaning is in the text—you may

---

Readers interpret a work informally among friends; however, when representatives of different schools of literary theory are asked, "What is this work really about?" they often respond with answers particular to their theoretical approach—so that *Hamlet* can be about anything from the breakdown of Elizabethan society to men's fears of feminine sexuality. French Romantic painter Eugène Delacroix illustrates Act 5, Scene 1, with his 1839 work *Hamlet and Horatio in the Graveyard*.

have intended to say *x*, but what you said actually means *y*—as if meaning were the product of the language itself. Sometimes we say context is what determines meaning: to know what this particular utterance means, you have to look at the circumstances or the historical context in which it figures. Some critics claim, as I have mentioned, that the meaning of a text is the experience of the reader. Intention, text, context, reader—what determines meaning?

Now the very fact that arguments are made for all four factors shows that meaning is complex and elusive, not something once and for all determined by any one of these factors. A long-standing argument in literary theory concerns the role of intention in the determination of literary meaning. A famous article called "The Intentional Fallacy" argues that for literary works arguments about interpretation are not settled by consulting the oracle (the author). The meaning of a work is not what the writer had in mind at some moment during composition of the work, or what the writer thinks the work means after it is finished, but, rather, what he or she succeeded in embodying in the work. If in ordinary conversation we often treat the meaning of an utterance as what the utterer intends, it is because we are more interested in what the speaker is thinking at that moment than in his or her words, but literary works are valued for the particular structures of words that they have put into circulation. Restricting the meaning of a work to what an author might have intended remains a possible critical strategy, but usually these days such meaning is tied not to an inner intention but to analysis of the author's personal or historical circumstances: what sort of act was this author performing, given the situation of the moment? This strategy denigrates later responses to the work, suggesting that the work answers the concerns of its moment of creation and only accidentally the concerns of subsequent readers.

Critics who defend the notion that intention determines meaning seem to fear that if we deny this, we place readers above authors and decree that "anything goes" in interpretation. But if you come up with an interpretation, you have to persuade others of its pertinence, or else it will be dismissed. No one claims that "anything goes." As for authors, isn't it better to honor them for the power of their creations to stimulate endless thought and give rise to a variety of readings than for what we imagine to be a work's original meaning? None of this is to say that authors' statements about a work have no interest: for many critical projects they are especially valuable, as texts to juxtapose with the text of the work. They may be crucial, for example, in analyzing the thought of an author or discussing the ways in which a work might have complicated or subverted an announced view or intention.

The meaning of a work is not what the author had in mind at some point, nor is it simply a property of the text or the experience of a reader. Meaning is an inescapable notion because it is not something simple or simply determined. It is simultaneously an experience of a subject and a property of a text. It is both what we understand and what *in* the text we *try* to understand. Arguments about meaning are always possible, and in that sense meaning is undecided, always to be decided, subject to decisions which are never irrevocable. If we must adopt some overall principle or formula, we might say that meaning is determined by context, since context includes rules of language, the situation of the author and the reader, and anything else that might conceivably be relevant. But if we say that meaning is context bound, then we must add that context is boundless: there is no determining in advance what might count as relevant, what enlarging of context might be able to shift what we regard as the meaning of a text. Meaning is context bound, but context is boundless.

Major shifts in the interpretation of literature brought about by theoretical discourses might, in fact, be thought of as the result of the widening or redescription of context. For example, Toni Morrison argues that American literature has been deeply marked by the often unacknowledged historical presence of slavery, and that this literature's engagements with freedom—the freedom of the frontier, of the open road, of the unfettered imagination—should be read in the context of enslavement, from which they take significance. And Edward Said has suggested that Jane Austen's novels should be interpreted against a background which is excluded from them: the exploitation of the colonies of the empire which provides the wealth to support a decorous life at home in Britain. Meaning is context bound, but context is boundless, always open to mutations under the pressure of theoretical discussions.

Accounts of hermeneutics frequently distinguish a *hermeneutics of recovery*, which seeks to reconstruct the original context of production (the circumstances and intentions of the author and the meanings a text might have had for its original readers), from a *hermeneutics of suspicion*, which seeks to expose the unexamined assumptions on which a text may rely (political, sexual, philosophical, linguistic). The first may celebrate the text and its author as it seeks to make an original message accessible to readers today, while the second is often said to deny the authority of the text. But these associations are not fixed and can well be reversed: a hermeneutics of recovery, in restricting the text to some supposedly original meaning remote from our concerns, may reduce its power, while a hermeneutics of suspicion may value the text for the way in which, unbeknownst to its author, it engages and helps us to rethink issues of moment today (perhaps subverting assumptions of its author in the process). More pertinent than this distinction may be a distinction between (1) interpretation which takes

Toni Morrison, author of *Beloved*, for which she won the Nobel Prize in Literature, has argued that the United States' literature of freedom should be read in the context of the nation's history of slavery, which gives it significance.

the text, in its functioning, to have something valuable to say (this might be either reconstructive or suspicious hermeneutics) and (2) "symptomatic" interpretation which treats the text as the symptom of something non-textual, something supposedly "deeper," which is the real source of interest, be it the psychic life of the author or the social tensions of an era or the homophobia of bourgeois society. Symptomatic interpretation neglects the specificity of the object—it is a sign of something else—and so is not very satisfying as a mode of interpretation, but when it focuses on the cultural practice of which the work is an instance, it can be useful to an account of that practice. Interpreting a poem as a symptom or instance of features of the lyric, for example, might be unsatisfactory hermeneutics but a useful contribution to poetics. To this I now turn.

FIVE

Rhetoric, Poetics, and Poetry

●

POETICS I HAVE DEFINED AS THE ATTEMPT to account for literary effects by describing the conventions and reading operations that make them possible. It is closely allied to *rhetoric*, which since classical times has been the study of the persuasive and expressive resources of language: the techniques of language and thought that can be used to construct effective discourses. Aristotle separated rhetoric from poetics, treating rhetoric as the art of persuasion and poetics as the art of imitation or representation. Medieval and Renaissance traditions, though, assimilated the two: rhetoric became the art of eloquence, and poetry (since it seeks to teach, to delight, and to move) was a superior instance of this art. In the

Plato, who banned poetry from his ideal republic, and Aristotle, who recognized the form as an important outlet for passionate feelings, disagreed on the value of this potentially incendiary, potentially liberating mode of expression. This marble panel by fifteenth-century artist Luca Della Robbia showing the two philosophers in debate is from the north side of the lower basement of the bell tower at the Museo dell'Opera del Duomo in Florence, Italy.

nineteenth century, rhetoric came to be seen as artifice divorced from the genuine activities of thought or of poetic imagination and fell into disfavor. In the late twentieth century rhetoric has been revived as the study of the structuring powers of discourse.

Poetry is related to rhetoric: poetry is language that makes abundant use of figures of speech and language that aims to be powerfully persuasive. And, ever since Plato excluded poets from his ideal republic, when poetry has been attacked or denigrated, it has been as deceptive or frivolous rhetoric that misleads citizens and calls up extravagant desires. Aristotle asserted the value of poetry by focusing on imitation (mimesis) rather than rhetoric. He argued that poetry provides a safe outlet for the release of intense emotions. And he claimed that poetry models the valuable experience of passing from ignorance to knowledge. (Thus, in the key moment of "recognition" in tragic drama, the hero realizes his error and spectators realize that "there but for the grace of God go I.") Poetics, as an account of the resources and strategies of literature, is not reducible to an account of rhetorical figures, but poetics could be seen as part of an expanded rhetoric that studies the resources for linguistic acts of all kinds.

Rhetorical Figures

Literary theory has been much concerned with rhetoric, and theorists debate the nature and function of rhetorical figures. A rhetorical figure has generally been defined as an alteration of or swerve from "ordinary" usage; for instance, "My love is a rose" uses *rose* to mean not the flower but something beautiful and precious (this is the figure of metaphor). Or "The Secret Sits" makes the secret an agent capable of sitting (personification). Rhetoricians formerly attempted to distinguish specific "tropes" which "turn" or alter the meaning of a word (as in metaphor) from more miscellaneous "figures" of indirection which arrange words to achieve special effects. Some figures are: alliteration (the repetition of a consonant); apostrophe (addressing something that is not a regular listener, as in "Be still, my heart!"); and assonance (the repetition of a vowel sound).

Recent theory rarely distinguishes *figure* from *trope* and has even questioned the notion of an "ordinary" or "literal" meaning from which figures or tropes swerve. For example, is the term *metaphor* itself literal or figurative? Jacques Derrida, in "White Mythology," shows how theoretical accounts of metaphor seem inevitably to rely on metaphors. Some theorists have even embraced the paradoxical conclusion that language is fundamentally figurative and that what we call literal language consists of figures whose figurative nature has been forgotten. When we talk of "grasping" a "hard problem," for instance, these two expressions become literal through the forgetting of their possible figurality.

From this perspective, it's not that there is no distinction between literal and figurative but rather that tropes and figures are fundamental structures of language, not exceptions and distortions. Traditionally, the most important figure has been metaphor. A metaphor treats something *as* something else (calling George a donkey or my love a red, red rose). Metaphor is thus a version of a basic way of knowing: we know something by seeing it *as* something. Theorists speak of "metaphors we live by," basic metaphorical schemes, like "life is a journey." Such schemes structure our ways of thinking about the world: we try to "get somewhere" in life, "find our way," "know where we're going," "encounter obstacles," and so on.

Metaphor has been treated as basic to language and the imagination because it is cognitively respectable, not inherently frivolous or ornamental. Its literary force, though, may depend on its incongruity. Wordsworth's phrase "the child is father of the man" stops you, makes you think, and then lets you see the relationship of generations in a new light: the child's relationship to the man he later becomes is compared to a father's relation to his child. Because a metaphor can carry an elaborate proposition, even a theory, it is the rhetorical figure most easily justified.

But theorists have also stressed the importance of other figures. For Roman Jakobson, metaphor and metonymy are the two fundamental structures of language: if metaphor links by means of similarity, metonymy links by means of contiguity. Metonymy moves from one thing to another that is contiguous with it, as when we say "the Crown" for "the Queen." Metonymy produces order by linking things in spatial and temporal series, moving from one thing to another within a given domain, rather than linking one domain to another, as metaphor can do. Other theorists add *synecdoche* and *irony* to complete a list of "four master tropes." Synecdoche is the substitution of part for whole: "ten hands" for "ten workers." It infers qualities of the whole from those of a part and allows parts to represent wholes. Irony juxtaposes appearance and reality; what happens is the opposite of what is expected (what if it rains on the weather forecaster's picnic?). These four master tropes—metaphor, metonymy, synecdoche, irony—are used by the historian Hayden White to analyze historical explanation or "emplotment" as he calls it: they are the basic rhetorical structures by which we make sense of experience. The fundamental idea of rhetoric as a discipline, which comes out well in this fourfold example, is that there are basic structures of language which underlie and make possible the meanings produced in a wide variety of discourses.

Genres

Literature depends on rhetorical figures but also on larger structures, particularly literary genres. What are genres and what is their role? Are terms like *epic* and *novel* simply convenient ways of classifying works on the basis of gross resemblances or do they have functions for readers and writers?

For readers, genres are sets of conventions and expectations: knowing whether we are reading a detective story or a romance, a lyric poem or a tragedy, we are on the lookout for different things and make assumptions about what will be significant. Reading a detective story, we look for clues in a way we don't when reading a tragedy. What would be a striking figure in a lyric—"the Secret sits in the middle"—might be a minor circumstantial detail in a ghost story or work of science fiction, where secrets might have acquired bodies.

Historically, many theorists of genre have followed the Greeks, who divided works among three broad classes according to who speaks: *poetic* or *lyric*, where the narrator speaks in the first person, *epic* or *narrative*, where the narrator speaks in his own voice but allows characters to speak in theirs, and *drama*, where the characters do all the talking. Another way of making this distinction is to focus on the relation of speaker to audience. In epic, there is oral recitation: a poet directly confronting the listening audience. In drama, the author is concealed from the audience and the characters on stage talk. In lyric—the most complicated case—the poet, in singing or chanting, turns his back on his listeners, so to speak, and "pretends to be talking to himself or to someone else: a spirit of Nature, a Muse, a personal friend, a lover, a god, a personified abstraction, or a natural object." To these three elementary genres we can add the modern genre of the novel, which addresses the reader through a book—a topic we'll take up in Chapter 6.

Epic and tragic drama were in ancient times and in the Renaissance the crowning achievements of literature, the highest accomplishments of any aspiring poet. The invention of the novel brought a new competitor

onto the literary scene, but between the late eighteenth century and the mid-twentieth century, the lyric, a short nonnarrative poem, came to be identified with the essence of literature. Once seen primarily as a mode of elevated expression, the elegant formulation of cultural values and attitudes, lyric poetry later came to be seen as the expression of powerful feeling, dealing at once with everyday life and transcendent values, giving concrete expression to the most inward feelings of the individual subject. This idea still holds sway. Contemporary theorists, though, have come to treat lyric less as expression of the poet's feelings and more as associative and imaginative work *on* language—an experimenting with linguistic connections and formulations that makes poetry a disruption of culture rather than the main repository of its values.

Poetry as Word and Act

Literary theory that is focused on poetry debates, among other things, the relative importance of different ways of viewing poems: a poem is both a structure made of words (a text) and an event (an act of the poet, an experience of the reader, an event in literary history). For the poem conceived as verbal construction, a major question is the relation between meaning and the nonsemantic features of language, such as sound and rhythm. How do the nonsemantic features of language work? What effects, conscious and unconscious, do they have? What sorts of interaction between semantic and nonsemantic features can be expected?

For the poem as act, a key question has been the relation between the act of the author who writes the poem and that of the speaker or "voice" that speaks there. This is a complicated matter. The author does not speak

The ancient Greeks divided works among three broad classes—poetic or lyric, epic or narrative, and drama. Austrian artist Gustav Klimt's rendering of ancient Greek lyric poet Sappho is from 1888–90.

the poem; to write it, the author imagines him- or herself or another voice speaking it. To read a poem—for instance, "The Secret Sits"—is to say the words, "We dance round in a ring and suppose . . ." The poem seems to be an utterance, but it is the utterance of a voice of indeterminate status. To read its words is to put yourself in the position of saying them or else to imagine another voice saying them—the voice, we often say, of a narrator or speaker constructed by the author. Thus we have, on the one hand, the historical individual, Robert Frost, and on the other, the voice of this particular utterance. Intermediary between those two figures is another figure: the image of poetic voice that emerges from the study of a range of poems by a single poet (in Frost's case, perhaps, that of a crusty, down-to-earth but reflective observer of rural life). The importance of these different figures varies from one poet to another and from one sort of critical study to another. But in thinking about lyric, it is crucial to *begin* with a distinction between the voice that speaks and the poet who made the poem, thus creating this figure of voice.

Lyric poetry, according to a well-known saying by John Stuart Mill, is utterance overheard. Now when we overhear an utterance that engages our attention, what we characteristically do is imagine or reconstruct a speaker and a context: identifying a tone of voice, we infer the posture, situations, concerns, and attitudes of a speaker (sometimes coinciding with what we know of the author, but often not). This has been the dominant approach to the lyric in the twentieth century, and a succinct justification might be that literary works are fictional imitations of real-world utterances. Lyrics, then, are fictional imitations of personal utterance. It is as if each poem began with the invisible words, "[For example, I or someone could say] My love is like a red, red rose," or "[For example, I or someone could say] We dance round in a ring and suppose. . . ." Interpreting the poem, then, is a matter of working out, from indications of the text and from our general knowledge about speakers and common situations, the nature of the speaker's attitudes. What might lead someone to speak thus? The dominant mode of appreciation of poetry in schools and universities has been to focus on the complexities of the speaker's attitude, on the poem as the dramatization of thoughts and feelings of a speaker whom one reconstructs.

This is a productive approach to the lyric, for many poems do present a speaker who is performing recognizable speech acts: meditating on the significance of an experience, chiding a friend or lover, expressing admiration or devotion, for example. But if we turn to the beginnings of some of the most famous lyrics, such as Shelley's "Ode to the West Wind" or Blake's "The Tiger," difficulties arise: "O wild West Wind, thou breath of Autumn's being!" or "Tiger, Tiger, burning bright / In the forests of the night." It is hard

to imagine what sort of situation would lead someone to speak in this way or what nonpoetic act they would be performing. The answer we are likely to come up with is that these speakers are getting carried away and waxing

Eighteenth-century poet and lyricist
Robert Burns, known in Scotland simply as "The Bard," is celebrated there annually on Burns Day, January 25, his birthday. Burns composed original works but also collected hundreds of folk songs. His "Auld Lang Syne" is traditionally sung on New Year's. This portrait is an etching that appeared in *The Poetry of Burns, Centenary Edition* in 1896.

poetical, extravagantly posturing. If we try to understand these poems as fictional imitations of ordinary speech acts, the act seems to be that of imitating poetry itself.

The Extravagance of Lyric

What such examples suggest is the extravagance of lyric. Not only do lyric poems seem willing to address almost anything in preference to an actual audience (the wind, a tiger, my soul); they do so in hyperbolic accents. Exaggeration is the name of the game here: the tiger is not just orange but "burning"; the wind is the very "breath of Autumn's being" and, later in the poem, savior and destroyer. Even sardonic poems are based on hyperbolic condensations, as when Frost reduces human activity to dancing round in a ring and treats the many forms of knowledge as "supposing."

We touch here on a major theoretical issue, a paradox that seems to lie at the core of lyric poetry. The extravagance of poetry includes its aspiration to what theorists since classical times have called the "sublime": a relation to what exceeds human capabilities of understanding, provokes awe or passionate intensity, gives the speaker a sense of something beyond the human. But this transcendent aspiration is linked to rhetorical figures such as *apostrophe*, the trope of addressing what is not an actual listener, *personification*, the attribution of human qualities to what is not human, and *prosopopoeia*, the granting of speech to inanimate objects. How can the highest aspirations of verse be linked to such rhetorical devices?

When lyrics swerve from or play upon the circuit of communication to address what is not really a listener—a wind, a tiger, or the heart—this is sometimes said to signify strong feeling that leads the speaker to burst out in speech. But the emotional intensity attaches especially to the act of address or invocation itself, which frequently wills a state of affairs and

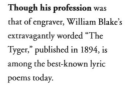

Though his profession was that of engraver, William Blake's extravagantly worded "The Tyger," published in 1894, is among the best-known lyric poems today.

attempts to call it into being by asking inanimate objects to bend themselves to the speaker's desire. "O lift me as a wave, a leaf, a cloud," Shelley's speaker urges the West Wind. The hyperbolic demand that the universe hear you and act accordingly is a move by which speakers constitute themselves as sublime poets or as visionary: someone who can address Nature and to whom it might respond. The "O" of invocation is a figure of poetic vocation, a move by which the speaking voice claims to be not a mere speaker of verse but an embodiment of poetic tradition and of the spirit of poetry. Calling winds to blow or calling for the unborn to hear your cries is an act of poetic ritual. It is ritualistic, in that the winds do not come and the unborn do not hear. Voice calls in order to be calling. It calls in order to dramatize voice: to summon images of its power so as to establish its identity as poetic and prophetic voice. The impossible, hyperbolic imperatives of apostrophes evoke poetic events, things that will be accomplished, if they are accomplished at all, in the event of the poem.

Narrative poems recount an event; lyrics, we might say, strive to be an event. But there is no guarantee that the poem will work, and apostrophe—as my brief quotations indicate—is what is most blatantly, most embarrassingly "poetical," most mystificatory and vulnerable to dismissal as hyperbolic nonsense. "Lift me as a wave, a leaf, a cloud!" Sure. Pull the other one. To be a poet is to strive to bring this sort of thing off, to wager that it won't be dismissed as a lot of nonsense.

English Romantic poet Percy Bysshe Shelley, here shown in a hand-colored woodcut, was an associate of both John Keats and Lord Byron. He published "Ode to the West Wind" in 1820, just two years before his death at the age of twenty-nine.

A major problem for the theory of poetry, as I've said, is the relation between the poem as a structure made of words and the poem as event. Apostrophes both attempt to make something happen and expose that happening as based on verbal devices—as on the empty "O" of apostrophic address: "O wild West Wind!"

To stress apostrophe, personification, prosopopoeia, and hyperbole is to join the theorists who through the ages have emphasized what *distinguishes* the lyric from other speech acts, what makes it the most literary of forms. The lyric, Northrop Frye writes, "is the genre that most clearly shows the hypothetical core of literature, narrative and meaning in their literal aspects as word-order and word-pattern." That is, lyric shows us meaning or story emerging from verbal patterning. You repeat words that echo in a rhythmical structure and see if story or sense won't emerge.

Rhythmic Words

Frye, whose *Anatomy of Criticism* is an invaluable compendium of thinking about lyric and other genres, calls the basic constituents of lyric *babble* and *doodle*, whose roots are *charm* and *riddle*. Poems babble, foregrounding nonsemantic features of language—sound, rhythm, repetition of letters—to produce charm or incantation:

> *This darksome burn, horseback brown,*
> *His rollrock highroad roaring down . . .*

Poems doodle or riddle us, in their wayward indirection, their puzzling formulations: what is a "rollrock highroad"? What of the Secret that "sits in the middle and knows"?

Such features are very prominent in nursery rhymes and ballads, where frequently pleasure lies in rhythm, incantation, and strangeness of image:

> *Pease porridge hot,*
> *Pease porridge cold,*
> *Pease porridge in the pot,*
> *Nine days old.*

The rhythmical pattern and the rhyme scheme flaunt the organization of this piece of language and can both provoke special interpretive attention (as when rhyme raises the question of relation of the rhyme words) and suspend inquiry: poetry has its own order which gives pleasure, so there's no need to ask about meaning; the rhythmical organization lets language get under the guard of intelligence and lodge itself in mechanical memory. We remember "Pease porridge hot" without bothering to inquire what pease porridge might be, and even if we find out we are likely to forget that before we forget "Pease porridge hot."

The foregrounding and making strange of language through metrical organization and repetition of sounds is the basis of poetry. Theories of poetry then posit relations between different types of organization of language—metrical, phonological, semantic, thematic—or, to put it most generally, between the semantic and nonsemantic dimensions of language, between what the poem says and how it says it. The poem is a structure of signifiers that absorbs and reconstitutes the signifieds, in that its formal patterns have effects on its semantic structures, assimilating the meanings words have in other contexts and subjecting them to new organization, altering stress and focus, shifting literal meanings to figurative ones, bringing terms into alignment, according to patterns of parallelism. It is the scandal of poetry that "contingent" features of sound and rhythm systematically infect and affect thought.

Interpreting Poems

At this level, the lyric is based on a convention of unity and autonomy, as if there were a rule: don't treat the poem as we might a bit of conversation, a fragment that needs a larger context to explain it, but assume that it has a structure of its own. Try to read it as if it were an aesthetic whole. The tradition of poetics makes available various theoretical models. The Russian Formalists of the early twentieth century posit that one level of structure in a poem should mirror another; Romantic theorists and English and American New Critics draw an analogy between poems and natural organisms: all the parts of the poem should fit together harmoniously. Poststructuralist readings posit an ineluctable tension between what poems do and what they say, the impossibility for a poem, or perhaps any piece of language, to practice what it preaches.

Recent conceptions of poems as intertextual constructions stress that poems are energized by echoes of past poems—echoes which they may not master. Unity becomes less a property of poems than something interpreters seek, whether they look for harmonious fusion or unresolved tension. To do this, readers identify oppositions in the poem (as between "us" and the Secret or between knowing and supposing) and see how other elements of the poem, particularly figurative expressions, align themselves with these oppositions.

Take Ezra Pound's famous two-line poem, "In a Station of the Metro":

> *The apparition of these faces in the crowd;*
> *Petals on a wet, black bough.*

Modernist poet Ezra Pound was born in America but lived much of his life abroad. His receipt of the Bollingen Prize in 1948 for his *Pisan Cantos* created much controversy, as he was known at the time as a traitor to his country (he was a fascist sympathizer during World War II).

Interpreting this involves working with the contrast between crowds in the subway and the natural scene. The pairing of the two lines enforces the parallel between the faces in the darkness of the subway and the petals on the black bough of a tree. But what then? The interpretation of poems depends not just on the convention of unity but also on the convention of significance: the rule is that poems, however slight in appearance, are supposed to be about something important, and therefore concrete details should be taken to have general significance. They should be read as the sign or "objective correlative," to use T. S. Eliot's term, for important feelings or intimations of significance.

To make the opposition in Pound's little poem significant, readers need to reflect on how the parallel might work. Is the poem *contrasting* the urban crowd scene in the metro with the peaceful natural scene of petals on a wet tree limb or is it *equating* them, noting a similarity? Both options are possible, but the latter seems to make possible a richer reading by prompting a step powerfully underwritten by the tradition of poetic interpretation. The perception of *resemblance* between faces in the crowd and petals on a bough—seeing faces in the crowd as petals on a bough—is an instance of the poetic imagination "seeing the world anew," grasping unexpected relationships and, perhaps, appreciating what to other observers would be trivial or oppressive, finding profundity in formal appearance. This little poem thus can become a reflection on the power of poetic imagination to achieve the effects that the poem itself achieves. An example like this illustrates a basic convention of poetic interpretation: consider what this poem and its procedures say about poetry or the creation of meaning. Poems, in their deployment of rhetorical operations, may be read as explorations in poetics, just as novels, as we shall see next, are at some level reflections on the making intelligible of our experience of time and are thus explorations in narrative theory.

SIX

Narrative

•

ONCE UPON A TIME, *literature* meant above all poetry. The novel was a modern upstart, too close to biography or chronicle to be genuinely literary, a popular form that could not aspire to the high callings of lyric and epic poetry. But in the twentieth century the novel has eclipsed poetry, both as what writers write and what readers read and, since the 1960s, narrative has come to dominate literary education as well. People still study poetry—often, it is required—but novels and short stories have become the core of the curriculum.

This is not just a result of the preferences of a mass readership, who happily pick up stories but seldom read poems. Literary and cultural theory have increasingly claimed cultural centrality for narrative. Stories, the argument goes, are the main way we make sense of things, whether

Life follows not scientific logic, but the logic of story, of narrative. We use this narrative logic, theorists argue, to make sense of our lives and the wider world.

in thinking of our lives as a progression leading somewhere or in telling ourselves what is happening in the world. Scientific explanation makes sense of things by placing them under laws—whenever *a* and *b* obtains, *c* will occur—but life is generally not like that. It follows not a scientific logic of cause and effect but the logic of story, where to understand is to conceive of how one thing leads to another, how something might have come about: how Maggie ended up selling software in Singapore, how George's father came to give him a car.

We make sense of events through possible stories; philosophers of history, I mentioned in Chapter 2, have even argued that the historical explanation follows not the logic of scientific causality but the logic of story: to understand the French Revolution is to grasp a narrative showing how one event led to another. Narrative structures are pervasive: Frank Kermode notes that when we say a ticking clock goes "tick-tock," we give the noise a fictional structure, differentiating between two physically identical sounds, to make *tick* a beginning and *tock* an end. "The clock's *tick-tock* I take to be a model of what we call a plot, an organization that humanizes time by giving it form."

The theory of narrative ("narratology") has been an active branch of literary theory, and literary study relies on theories of narrative structure: on notions of plot, of different kinds of narrators, of narrative techniques. The poetics of narrative, as we might call it, both attempts to understand the components of narrative and analyzes how particular narratives achieve their effects.

But narrative is not just an academic subject. There is a basic human drive to hear and tell stories. Children very early develop what one might call a basic narrative competence: demanding stories, they know when you are trying to cheat by stopping before reaching the end. So the first question for the theory of narrative might be, what do we implicitly know about the basic shape of stories that enables us to distinguish between a story that ends "properly" and one that doesn't, where things are left hanging? The theory of narrative might, then, be conceived as an attempt to spell out, to make explicit, this narrative competence, just as linguistics is an attempt to make explicit linguistic competence: what speakers of a language unconsciously know in knowing a language. Theory here can be conceived as a setting forth of an intuitive cultural knowledge or understanding.

Plot

What are the elemental requirements of a story? Aristotle says that plot is the most basic feature of narrative, that good stories must have a beginning, middle, and end, and that they give pleasure because of the rhythm of their ordering. But what creates the impression that a particular series of events has this shape? Theorists have proposed various accounts. Essentially, though, a plot requires a transformation. There must be an initial situation, a change involving some sort of reversal, and a resolution that marks the change as significant. Some theories emphasize types of parallelism that produce satisfactory plots, such as the move from one relationship between characters to its opposite, or from a fear or prediction to its realization or its inversion; from a problem to its solution, or from a false accusation or misrepresentation to its rectification. In each case we find the association of a development on the level of events with a transformation on the level of theme. A mere sequence of events does not make a story. There must be an end relating back to the beginning— according to some theorists, an end that indicates what has happened to the desire that led to the events the story narrates.

If narrative theory is an account of narrative competence, it must focus also on readers' ability to identify plots. Readers can tell that two works are versions of the same story; they can summarize plots and discuss the adequacy of a plot summary. It's not that they will always agree, but disagreements are likely to reveal considerable shared understanding. The theory of narrative postulates the existence of a level of structure—what we generally call "plot"—independent of any particular language or representational medium. Unlike poetry, which gets lost in translation, plot can be preserved in translation from one language or one medium into another: a silent film or a comic strip can have the same plot as a short story.

We discover, though, that there are two ways of thinking about plot. From one angle, plot is a way of shaping events to make them into a genuine story: writers and readers shape events into a plot in their attempts to make sense of things. From another angle, plot is what gets shaped by narratives, as they present the same "story" in different ways. So a sequence of acts by three characters can be shaped (by writers and readers) into the elementary plot of heterosexual love, where a young man seeks to wed a young woman, their desire is resisted by paternal opposition, but some twist of events allows the young lovers to come together. This plot with three characters can be presented in narrative from the point of view of the suffering heroine, or the angry father, or the young man, or an external observer puzzled by these events, or an omniscient narrator who can describe each character's innermost feelings or who takes a knowing distance from these goings-on. From this angle, the plot or story is the given and the discourse is the varied presentations of it.

The three levels I have been discussing—events, plot (or story), and discourse—function as two oppositions: between events and plot, and between story and discourse.

events/plot

    story/discourse

Plot or story is the material that is presented, ordered from a certain point of view by discourse (different versions of "the same story"). But plot itself is already a shaping of events. A plot can make a wedding the happy ending of the story or the beginning of a story—or can make it a turn in the middle. What readers actually encounter, though, is the discourse of a text: the plot is something readers *infer* from the text, and the idea of elementary events out of which this plot was formed is also an inference or construction of the reader. If we talk about events that have been shaped into a plot, it is to highlight the meaningfulness and organization of the plot.

Presentation

The basic distinction of the theory of narrative, then, is between plot and presentation, story and discourse. (The terminology varies from one theorist to another.) Confronted with a text (a term that includes films and other representations), the reader makes sense of it by identifying the story and then seeing the text as one particular presentation of that story; by identifying "what happens," we are able to think of the rest of the verbal material as the way of portraying what takes place. Then we can ask what type of presentation has been chosen and what difference that makes. There are many variables, and they are crucial to narratives' effects. Much narrative theory explores different ways of conceiving these variables. Here are some key questions that identify meaningful variation.

    Who speaks? By convention every narrative is said to have a narrator, who may stand outside the story or be a character within it. Theorists distinguish "first-person narration," where a narrator says "I," from what is somewhat confusingly called "third-person narration," where there is no "I"—the narrator is not identified as a character in the story and all the characters are referred to in the third person, by name or as "he" or "she." First-person narrators may be the main *protagonists* of the story they tell; they may be *participants*, minor characters in the story; or they may be *observers* of the story, whose function is not to act but to describe things to us. First-person observers may be fully developed as individuals with a name, history, and personality, or they may not be developed at all and quickly drop from sight as the narration gets under way, effacing themselves after introducing the story.

Who speaks to whom? The author creates a text which is read by readers. Readers infer from the text a narrator, a voice which speaks. The narrator addresses listeners who are sometimes implied or constructed, sometimes explicitly identified (especially in stories within stories, where one character becomes the narrator and tells the inner story to other characters). The narrator's audience is often called the *narratee*. Whether or not narratees are explicitly identified, the narrative implicitly constructs an audience by what its narration takes for granted and what it explains. A work from another time and place usually implies an audience that recognizes certain references and shares certain assumptions that a modern reader may not share. Feminist criticism has been especially interested in the way that European and American narratives frequently posit a male reader: the reader is implicitly addressed as one who shares a masculine view.

Who speaks when? Narration may be situated at the time at which events occur (as in Alain Robbe-Grillet's *Jealousy*, where narration takes the form "now *x* is happening, now *y* is happening, now *z* is happening"). Telling may immediately follow particular events, as in epistolary novels

(novels in the form of letters), such as Samuel Richardson's *Pamela*, where each letter deals with what had happened up to that point. Or, as is most common, narration may occur after the final events in the narrative, as the narrator looks back on the entire sequence.

Who speaks what language? Narrative voices may have their own distinctive language, in which they recount everything in the story, or they may adopt and report the language of others. A narrative that sees things through the consciousness of a child may either use adult language to report the child's perceptions or slip into a child's language. The Russian theorist Mikhail Bakhtin describes the novel as fundamentally polyphonic (multi-voiced) or dialogic rather than monological (single-voiced): the essence of the novel is its staging of different voices or discourses and, thus, of the clash of social perspectives and points of view.

Who speaks with what authority? To tell a story is to claim a certain authority, which listeners grant. When the narrator of Jane Austen's *Emma* begins, "Emma Woodhouse, handsome, clever, and rich, with a comfortable home and happy disposition, . . ." we don't sceptically wonder whether she really was handsome and clever. We accept this statement until we are given reason to think otherwise. Narrators are sometimes termed *unreliable* when they provide enough information about situations and clues about their own biases to make us doubt their interpretations of events, or when we find reasons to doubt that the narrator shares the same values as the author. Theorists speak of *self-conscious narration* when narrators discuss the fact that they are telling a story, hesitate about how to tell it, or even flaunt the fact that they can determine how the story will turn out. Self-conscious narration highlights the problem of narrative authority.

Focalization

Who sees? Discussions of narrative frequently speak of the "point of view from which a story is told," but this use of *point of view* confuses two separate questions: who speaks? and whose vision is presented? Henry James's novel *What Maisie Knew* employs a narrator who is not a child but it presents the story through the consciousness of the child Maisie. Maisie is not the narrator; she is described in the third person, as "she," but the novel presents many things from her perspective. Maisie, for example, does not fully understand the sexual dimension of relations between the adults around her. The story is, to use a term developed by the theorists of narrative Mieke Bal and Gérard Genette, *focalized* through her. Hers is the consciousness or position through which events are brought into focus. The question "Who speaks?," then, is separate from the question of "Who sees?" From whose perspective are the events brought into focus and presented? The focalizer may or may not be the same as the narrator. There are numerous variables here.

- **TEMPORAL.** Narration may focalize events from the time at which they occurred, from shortly afterward, or from long afterward. It may focus on what the focalizer knew or thought at the time of the event or how she saw things later, with the benefit of hindsight. In recounting something that happened to her as a child, a narrator may focalize the event through the consciousness of the child she was, restricting the account to what she thought and felt at the time, or she may focalize events through her

Samuel Richardson, who in his youth was a prolific storyteller and letter writer, even penning letters for young women to their hopeful lovers, became a printer and publisher but did not publish his own epistolary first novel, *Pamela* (1740), until he was fifty-one. *Pamela* tells the tale of the heroine's life through a series of letters that relate the action up to the point each letter is written.

PAMELA

E. F. Burney del.   Walker sculp.

Plate X.   Published as the Act directs by Harrison & Cº Decʳ 10. 1785.

knowledge and understanding at the time of narration. Or, of course, she may combine these perspectives, moving between what she knew or felt then and what she recognizes now. When third-person narration focalizes events through a particular character, it can employ similar variations, recounting how things seemed to the character at the time or how they are perceived later. The choice of temporal focalization makes an enormous difference in a narrative's effects. Detective stories, for instance, recount only what the focalizer knew at each moment of the investigation, saving the knowledge of the outcome for the climax.

- **DISTANCE AND SPEED.** The story may be focalized through a microscope, as it were, or through a telescope, proceeding slowly with great detail or quickly telling us what happened: "The grateful Monarch gave the Prince his daughter's hand in marriage, and when the King died, the Prince succeeded to the throne and reigned happily for many years." Related to speed are variations in frequency: we can be told what happened on a particular occasion or what happened every Thursday. Most distinctive is what Gérard Genette calls the "pseudo-iterative," in which something so specific that it could not happen over and over is presented as what regularly happened.

- **LIMITATIONS OF KNOWLEDGE.** At one extreme, a narrative may focalize the story through a very limited perspective—a "camera's eye" or "fly-on-the-wall" perspective—recounting actions without giving us access to characters' thoughts. Even here, great variations can occur depending on what degree of understanding "objective" or "external"

Despite the claim of Jane Austen's authoritative narrator in *Emma* that the heroine has the advantages of being not only handsome but clever and rich as well, Emma Woodhouse makes a series of embarrassing social blunders. In the end, however, she is graced with the advantage of good fortune as well, as ultimately she finds love and protection in marriage to her friend and mentor, George Knightley.

He stopped to look the question.

descriptions imply. Thus, "the old man lit a cigarette" seems focalized through an observer familiar with human activities, whereas "the human with whitish hairs on the top of his head held a flaming stick close to him, and smoke began to rise from a white tube attached to his body" seems focalized through a space alien or person who is very "spaced out." At the other extreme lies what is called "omniscient narration" where the focalizer is a godlike figure who has access to the innermost thoughts and hidden motives of the characters: "The king was pleased beyond measure at the sight, but his greed for gold was still not satisfied." Omniscient narration, where there seem in principle no limitations on what can be known and told, is common not only in traditional tales but in modern novels, where the choice of what will actually be told is crucial.

Stories focalized primarily through the consciousness of a single character occur both in first-person narration, where the narrator tells what he or she thought and observed, and in third-person narration, where it is often called "third-person limited point of view," as in *What Maisie Knew*. *Unreliable narration* can result from limitations of point of view—when we gain a sense that the consciousness through which focalization occurs is unable or unwilling to understand the events as competent story-readers would.

These and other variations in narration and focalization do much to determine the overall effect of novels. A story with omniscient narration, detailing the feelings and hidden motivations of protagonists and displaying knowledge of how events will turn out, may give the impression of the comprehensibility of the world. It may highlight, for example, the contrast between what people intend and what inevitably happens ("Little did he know that two hours later he would be

In *What Maisie Knew,* American expatriate and prolific writer Henry James employed narrative focalization; although he refers to his protagonist, the child Maisie, in the third person, he tells the story from her point of view.

run over by a carriage and all his plans come to naught"). A story told from the *limited* point of view of a single protagonist may highlight the utter unpredictability of what happens: since we don't know what other characters are thinking or what else is going on, everything that occurs to this character may be a surprise. The complications of narrative are further heightened by the embedding of stories within other stories, so that the act of telling a story becomes an event in the story—an event whose consequences and significance become a principal concern. Stories within stories within stories.

What Stories Do

Theorists also discuss the function of stories. I mentioned in Chapter 2 that "narrative display texts," a class which includes both literary narratives and stories people tell one another, circulate because their stories are tellable, "worth it." Storytellers are always warding off the potential question, "So what?" But what makes a story "worth it"? What do stories do?

First, they give pleasure—pleasure, Aristotle tells us, through their imitation of life and their rhythm. The narrative patterning that produces a twist, as when the biter is bitten or the tables are turned, gives pleasure in itself, and many narratives have essentially this function: to amuse listeners by giving a new twist to familiar situations.

The pleasure of narrative is linked to desire. Plots tell of desire and what befalls it, but the movement of narrative itself is driven by desire in the form of "epistemophilia," a desire to know: we want to discover secrets, to know the end, to find the truth. If what drives narrative is the "masculine" urge to mastery, the desire to unveil the truth (the "naked truth"), then what of the knowledge that narrative offers us to satisfy that wish? Is that knowledge itself an effect of desire? Theorists ask such questions about the links between desire, stories, and knowledge.

For stories also have the function, as theorists have emphasized, of teaching us about the world, showing us how it works, enabling us—through the devices of focalization—to see things from other vantage points, and to understand others" motives that in general are opaque to us. The novelist E. M. Forster observes that in offering the possibility of perfect knowledge of others, novels compensate for our dimness about others in "real" life. Characters in novels

.

are people whose secret lives are visible or might be visible: we are people whose secret lives are invisible. And that is why novels, even when they are about wicked people, can solace us; they suggest a more comprehensible and thus a more manageable human race, they give us the illusion of perspicacity and of power.

Through the knowledge they present, narratives police. Novels in the Western tradition show how aspirations are tamed and desires adjusted to social reality. Many novels are the story of youthful illusions crushed. They tell us of desire, provoke desire, lay down for us the scenarios of heterosexual desire, and, since the eighteenth century, they have increasingly

In novelist E. M. Forster's
A Room with a View, we are given a glimpse into the inner life of Lucy Honeychurch, who is caught between her own passionate nature and the middle-class repression represented by her chaperone, Miss Bartlett, played by Dame Maggie Smith in the Oscar-winning 1985 Merchant-Ivory production.

worked to suggest that we achieve our true identity, if at all, in love, in personal relations, rather than in public action. But as they coach us to believe that there is such a thing as "being in love," they also subject that idea to demystification.

Insofar as we become who we are through a series of identifications (see Chapter 8), novels are a powerful device for the internalization of social norms. But narratives also provide a mode of social criticism. They expose the hollowness of worldly success, the world's corruption, its failure to meet our noblest aspirations. They expose the predicaments of the oppressed, in stories that invite readers, through identification, to see certain situations as intolerable.

Finally, the basic question for theory in the domain of narrative is this: is narrative a fundamental form of knowledge (giving knowledge of the world through its sense making) or is it a rhetorical structure that distorts as much as it reveals? Is narrative a source of knowledge or of illusion? Is the knowledge it purports to present a knowledge that is the effect of desire? The theorist Paul de Man observes that while no one in his right mind would try to grow grapes by the light of the word *day*, we find it very hard indeed to avoid conceiving of our lives by patterns of fictional narratives. Does this imply that narratives' clarifying and consoling effects are delusory?

To answer these questions we would need both knowledge of the world that is *independent* of narratives and some basis for deeming this knowledge more authoritative than what narratives provide. But whether there is such authoritative knowledge separate from narrative is precisely what's at stake in the question of whether narrative is a source of knowledge or of illusion. So it seems likely that we cannot answer this question, if indeed it has an answer. Instead we must move back and forth between awareness of narrative as a rhetorical structure that produces the illusion of perspicacity and a study of narrative as the principal kind of sense making at our disposal. After all, even the exposure of narrative as rhetoric has the structure of a narrative: it is a story in which our initial delusion yields to the harsh light of truth and we emerge sadder but wiser, disillusioned but chastened. We stop dancing around and contemplate the secret. So the story goes.

SEVEN

Performative Language

IN THIS CHAPTER I PURSUE AN INSTANCE of "theory" by following a concept that has flourished in literary and cultural theory and whose fortunes illustrate the way ideas change as they are drawn into the realm of "theory." The problem of "performative" language brings into focus important issues concerning meaning and effects of language and leads to questions about identity and the nature of the subject.

Austin's Performatives

The concept of performative utterance was developed in the 1950s by the British philosopher J. L. Austin. He proposed a distinction between two sorts of utterances: *constative* utterances, such as "George promised to

Performative utterances—such as "I christen thee . . ."—do not describe the action they designate; they perform it. In this 1943 photograph, Rachel Stevenson christens the first ship conceived and constructed by an all–African American labor force on the East Coast. Stevenson, the sponsor of the ship, was an employee for almost twenty years of the company that built it.

come," make a statement, describe a state of affairs, and are true or false. *Performative* utterances, or *performatives*, are not true or false and actually perform the action to which they refer. To say "I promise to pay you" is not to describe a state of affairs but to perform the act of promising; the utterance is itself the act. Austin writes that when, in a wedding ceremony, the priest or civil official asks, "Do you take this woman to be your lawful wedded wife?" and I respond "I do," I do not describe anything, I do it; "I am not reporting on a marriage: I am indulging in it." When I say "I do," this performative utterance is neither true nor false. It may be appropriate or inappropriate, depending on the circumstances; it may be "felicitous" or "infelicitous" in Austin's terminology. If I say "I do," I may not succeed in marrying—if, for example, I am married already or if the person performing the ceremony is not authorized to perform weddings in this community. The utterance will "misfire," says Austin. The utterance will be unhappy—infelicitous—and so, no doubt, will the bride or groom, or perhaps both.

Performative utterances do not describe but perform the action they designate. It is in pronouncing these words that I promise, order, or marry. A simple test for the performative is the possibility of adding "hereby" in English before the verb, where *hereby* means "by uttering these words": "I hereby promise"; "We hereby declare our independence"; "I hereby order you . . ."; but not "I hereby walk to town." I can't perform the act of walking by pronouncing certain words.

The distinction between performative and constative captures an important difference between types of utterances and has the great virtue of alerting us to the extent to which language performs actions rather than merely reporting on them. But as Austin pushes further in his account of the performative, he encounters some difficulties. You can draw up a list of "performative verbs" which in the first person of the present indicative

(I promise, I order, I declare) perform the action they designate. But you can't define the performative by listing the verbs that behave in this way, because in the right circumstances you can perform the act of ordering someone to stop by shouting "Stop!" rather than "I hereby order you to stop." The apparently constative statement "I will pay you tomorrow," which certainly looks as though it will become either true or false, depending on what happens tomorrow, can, under the right conditions, be a *promise* to pay you, rather than a description or prediction like "*he* will pay you tomorrow." But once you allow for the existence of such "implicit performatives," where there is no explicitly performative verb, you have to admit that *any* utterance can be an implicit performative. The sentence "The cat is on the mat," your basic constative utterance, can be seen as the elliptical version of "I hereby affirm that the cat is on the mat," a performative utterance that accomplishes the act of affirming to which it refers. Constative utterances also perform actions—actions of stating, affirming, describing, and so on. They are, it turns out, a type of performative. This becomes significant at a later stage.

Performatives and Literature

Literary critics have embraced the notion of the performative as one that helps to characterize literary discourse. Theorists have long asserted that we must attend to what literary language *does* as much as to what it *says*, and the concept of the performative provides a linguistic and philosophical justification for this idea: there is a class of utterances that above all do something. Like the performative, the literary utterance does not refer to a prior state of affairs and is not true or false. The literary utterance too *creates* the state of affairs to which it refers, in several respects. First and most simply, it brings into being characters and their actions, for instance. The beginning of Joyce's *Ulysses*, "Stately plump Buck Mulligan came from the stairhead bearing a bowl of lather on which a mirror and a razor lay crossed," does not refer to some prior state of affairs but creates this character and this situation. Second, literary works bring into being ideas, concepts, which they deploy. La Rochefoucauld claims that no one would ever have thought of being in love if they hadn't read about it in books, and the notion of romantic love (and of its centrality to the lives of individuals) is arguably a massive literary creation. Certainly novels themselves, from *Don Quixote* to *Madame Bovary*, blame romantic ideas on other books.

In short, the performative brings to center stage a use of language previously considered marginal—an active, world-making use of language, which resembles literary language—and helps us to conceive of literature as act or event. The notion of literature as performative contributes to a defense of literature: literature is not frivolous pseudo-statements but takes its place among the acts of language that transform the world, bringing into being the things that they name.

The performative is linked with literature in a second way. In principle at least, the performative

James Joyce's *Ulysses*, placed by Modern Library at the top of its list of the best English-language novels of the twentieth century, employs literary utterance to create characters and situations. This image of Joyce appeared in a printed subscription order form for *Ulysses*, which was published in Paris in 1921.

breaks the link between meaning and the intention of the speaker, for what act I perform with my words is not determined by my intention but by social and linguistic conventions. The utterance, Austin insists, should not be considered as the outward sign of some inward act which it represents truly or falsely. If I say "I promise" under appropriate conditions, I have promised, have performed the act of promising, whatever intention I may have had in my head at the time. Since literary utterances are also events where the intention of the author is not thought to be what determines the meaning, the model of the performative seems highly pertinent.

But if literary language is performative and if a performative utterance is not true or false but felicitous or infelicitous, what does it mean for a literary utterance to be felicitous or infelicitous? This turns out to be a complicated matter. On the one hand, *felicity* may be just another name for what critics generally are interested in. Confronted with the opening of Shakespeare's sonnet "My mistress' eyes are nothing like the sun," we ask not whether this utterance is true or false, but what it does, how it fits in with the rest of the poem, and whether it works happily (felicitously) with the other lines. That might be one conception of felicity. But the model of the performative also directs our attention to the conventions that enable an utterance to be a promise or a poem—the conventions of the sonnet, say. The felicitousness of a literary utterance might thus involve its relation to the conventions of a genre. Does it comply and thus succeed in being a sonnet, rather than a misfire? But more than that, one might imagine, a literary composition is felicitous only when it fully becomes literature by being published, read, and accepted as a literary work, just as a bet becomes a bet only when it is accepted. In short, the notion of literature as performative enjoins us to reflect on the complex problem of what it is for a literary sequence to work.

Derrida's Performatives

The next key moment in the fortunes of the performative comes when Jacques Derrida takes up Austin's notion. Austin had distinguished between serious performatives which accomplish something, like promising or marrying, and "nonserious" utterances. His analysis, he says, applies to words spoken seriously: "I must not be joking, for example, or writing a poem. Our performative utterances, felicitous or not, are to be understood as issued in ordinary circumstances." But Derrida argues that what Austin sets aside in appealing to "ordinary circumstances" are the numerous ways in which bits of language can be repeated—"nonseriously" but also seriously, as an example or a quotation, for instance. This possibility of being repeated in new circumstances is essential to the nature of language; anything that couldn't be repeated in a "nonserious" fashion wouldn't be language but some mark inextricably tied to a physical situation. The possibility of repetition is basic to language, and performatives in particular can only work if they are recognized as versions of or quotations of regular formulas, such as "I do," or "I promise." (If the groom said "OK" rather than "I do," he might not succeed in marrying.) "Could a performative utterance succeed," asks Derrida, "if its formulation did not repeat a "codified" or iterable [repeatable] form, in other words if the formula that I utter to open a meeting, christen a boat, or undertake marriage were not identifiable as conforming to an iterable model, if it were not thus identifiable as a kind of citation?" Austin sets aside as anomalous, nonserious, or exceptional particular instances of what Derrida calls a "general iterability" that should be considered a law of language. "General" and fundamental, because, for something to be a sign, it must be able to be cited and repeated in all sorts of circumstances, including "nonserious" ones. Language is performative in the sense that

Algerian-born French philosopher Jacques Derrida, whose best-known work, *Of Grammatology,* was published in 1967, challenged Austin's failure to pursue his insights concerning classification of performatives and constantives.

it doesn't just transmit information but performs acts by its repetition of established discursive practices or ways of doing things. This will be important to the later fortunes of the performative.

Derrida also relates the performative to the general problem of acts that originate or inaugurate, acts that create something new, in the political as well as literary sphere. What is the relationship between a political act, like a declaration of independence, that creates a new situation, and literary utterances, that try to invent something new, in acts that are not constative statements but are performative, like promises? Both the political and the literary act depend on a complex, paradoxical combination of the performative and constative, where in order to succeed, the act must convince by referring to states of affairs but where success consists of bringing into being the condition to which it refers. Literary works claim to tell us about the world, but if they succeed they do so by bringing into being the characters and events they relate. Something similar is at work in inaugural acts in the political sphere. In the Declaration of Independence of the United States, for example, the key sentence runs: "We therefore . . . do solemnly publish and declare that these United colonies are and of right ought to be free and independent states." The declaration that these *are* independent states is a performative that is supposed to create the new reality to which it refers, but to support this claim is joined the constative assertion that they *ought* to be independent states.

Performative—Constative Relations

The tension between the performative and constative emerges clearly also in literature, where the difficulty Austin encounters of separating performative and constative can be seen as a crucial feature of the functioning of language. If every utterance is both performative and constative, including at least an implicit assertion of a state of affairs and a linguistic act, the relation between what an utterance says and what it does is not necessarily harmonious or cooperative. To see what is involved in the literary sphere, let us come back to Robert Frost's poem "The Secret Sits":

> *We dance round in a ring and suppose,*
> *But the Secret sits in the middle and knows.*

This poem depends on the opposition between supposing and knowing. To explore what attitude the poem takes to this opposition, what values it attaches to its opposing terms, we might ask whether the poem itself is in the mode of supposing or of knowing. Does the poem suppose, like "we" who dance round, or does it know, like the secret? We might imagine that, as a product of the human imagination, the poem would be an example of supposing, a case of dancing around, but its gnomic, proverbial character, and its confident declaration that the secret "knows," makes it seem very knowing indeed. So we can't be sure. But what does the poem show us about knowing? Well, the secret, which is something that one knows or does not know— thus, an *object* of knowing—here becomes by metonymy or contiguity the *subject* of knowing, *what knows* rather than *what is or is not known*. By capitalizing and personifying the entity, the Secret, the poem performs a rhetorical operation that promotes the object of knowledge to the position of subject. It thus shows us that a rhetorical supposition can produce the knower, can make the secret into a subject, a character in this little drama. The secret who knows is produced by an act of supposing, which moves the secret from the place of the object (*Someone knows a secret*) to the place of the subject (*The Secret knows*). The poem thus shows that its constative assertion, that the secret knows, depends on a performative supposing: the supposing that makes the secret into the subject supposed to know. The sentence *says* that the Secret knows but it *shows* that this is a supposition.

At this stage in the history of the performative, the contrast between constative and performative has been redefined: the constative is language claiming to represent things as they are, to name things that are already there, and the performative is the rhetorical operations, the acts of language, that undermine this claim by imposing linguistic categories, bringing things into being, organizing the world rather than simply representing what is. We can identify here what is called an "aporia" between performative and constative language. An "aporia" is the "impasse" of an undecidable oscillation, as when the chicken depends upon the egg but the egg depends on the chicken. The only way to claim that language functions performatively to shape the world is through a constative utterance, such as "Language shapes the world"; but contrariwise, there is no way to claim the constative transparency of language except by a speech act. The propositions which perform the act of stating necessarily claim to do nothing but merely display things as they are; yet if you want to show the contrary—that claims to represent things as they are in fact impose their categories on the world—you have no way to do this except through claims about what is or is not the case. The argument that the act of stating or describing is in fact performative must take the form of constative statements.

Butler's Performatives

The latest moment of this little history of the performative is the emergence of a "performative theory of gender and sexuality" in feminist theory and in gay and lesbian studies. The key figure here is the American philosopher Judith Butler, whose books *Gender Trouble: Feminism and the Subversion of Identity* (1990), *Bodies That Matter* (1993), and *Excitable Speech: A Politics of the Speech Act* (1997) have had great influence in the field of literary and cultural studies, particularly in feminist theory, and in the emerging field of gay and lesbian studies. The name "Queer Theory" has recently been adopted by the avant-garde of gay studies whose work in cultural theory is linked with political movements for gay liberation. It takes as its own name and throws back at society the most common insult that homosexuals encounter, the epithet "Queer!" The gamble is that flaunting this name can change its meaning and make it a badge of honor rather than an insult. Here a theoretical project is emulating

Members of the AIDS activist group ACT UP (AIDS Coalition to Unleash Power) block traffic on Broadway in New York City to protest the lack of health care and to celebrate the twentieth anniversary of the group's founding, March 29, 2007. ACT UP has used the epithet *queer* in its protests and demonstrations, changing the performative significance of a formerly oppressive epithet. For American philosopher Judith Butler, performatives are crucial to understanding social processes.

the tactics of the most visible activist organizations involved in the fight against AIDS—the group ACT UP, for instance, which in their demonstrations use such slogans as "We're here, we're queer, get used to it!"

Butler's *Gender Trouble* takes issue with the notion, common in American feminist writing, that a feminist politics requires a notion of feminine identity, of essential features which women share as women and which give them common interests and goals. For Butler, on the contrary, the fundamental categories of identity are cultural and social productions, more likely to be the *result* of political cooperation than its condition of possibility. They create the effect of the natural (remember Aretha Franklin's "You make me feel like a natural woman") and by imposing norms (definitions of what it is to be a woman) they threaten to exclude those who don't conform. In *Gender Trouble* Butler proposes that we consider gender as performative, in the sense that it is not what one is but what one does. A man is not what one is but something one does, a condition one enacts. Your gender is created by your acts, in the way that a promise is created by the act of promising. You become a man or a woman by repeated acts, which, like Austin's performatives, depend on social conventions, habitual ways of doing something in a culture. Just as there are regular, socially established ways of promising, making a bet, giving orders, and getting married, so there are socially established ways of being a man or being a woman.

This does not mean that gender is a choice, a role you put on, as you choose clothes to put on in the morning. That would suggest that there is an ungendered subject prior to gender who chooses, whereas in fact to be a subject at all is to be gendered: you can't, in this regime of gender, be a person without being male or female. "Subjected to gender but subjectivated [made a subject] by gender," writes Butler in *Bodies That Matter*, "the

'I' neither precedes nor follows the process of this gendering but emerges only within and as the matrix of gender relations themselves." Nor should the performativity of gender be thought of as a singular act, something accomplished by one particular act; rather, it is "the reiterative and citational practice," the compulsory repetition of gender norms that animate and constrain the gendered subject but which are also the resources from which resistance, subversions, and displacement are forged.

From this viewpoint, the utterance "It's a girl!" or "It's a boy!" by which a baby is, traditionally, welcomed into the world, is less a constative utterance (true or false, according to the situation) than the first in a long series of performatives that create the subject whose arrival

In this Currier & Ives lithograph, published in 1869, a husband sits by a child in a cradle and sews as a male servant does laundry. A well-dressed woman prepares to get into a carriage driven by another woman.

they announce. The naming of the girl initiates a continuous process of "girling," the making of a girl, through an "assignment" of compulsory repetition of gender norms, "the forcible citation of a norm." To be a subject at all is to be given this assignment of repetition, but—and this is important for Butler—an assignment which we never quite carry out according to expectation, so that we never quite inhabit the gender norms or ideals we are compelled to approximate. In that gap, in the different ways of carrying out the gender's "assignment," lie possibilities for resistance and change.

Stress falls here on the way the performative force of language comes from the repetition of prior norms, prior acts. So, the force of the insult "Queer!" comes not from the intention or authority of the speaker, who is most likely some fool quite unknown to the victim, but from the fact that the shout "Queer" repeats shouted insults of the past, interpellations or acts of address which produce the homosexual subject through reiterated shaming or abjection (abjection involves treating something as beyond the pale: "Anything but that!"). Butler writes,

> "Queer" derives its force precisely through the repeated . . . invocation by which a social bond among homophobic communities is formed through time. The interpellation echoes past interpellations, and binds the speakers, as if they spoke in unison across time. In this sense it is always an imaginary chorus that taunts "queer!"

What gives the insult its performative force is not the repetition itself but the fact that it is recognized as conforming to a model, a norm, and is linked with a history of exclusion. The utterance implies that the speaker is the spokesman for what is "normal" and works to constitute the addressee as deviant, beyond the pale. It is the repetition, the citation of a formula which is linked to norms sustaining a history of oppression, that gives a special force and viciousness to otherwise banal insults such as "nigger" or "kike." They accumulate the force of authority through the repetition or citation of a prior, authoritative set of practices, speaking as if with the voice of all the taunts of the past.

But the performative's link with the past implies the possibility of deflecting or redirecting the weight of the past, by attempting to capture and redirect the terms that carry an oppressive signification, as in the adoption of "queer" by homosexuals themselves. It's not that you become autonomous by choosing your name: names always carry historical weight and are subject to the uses others will make of them in the future. You can't control the terms that you choose to name yourselves. But the historical character of the performative process creates the possibility of a political struggle.

Stakes and Implications

Now it is obvious that the distance between the beginning and the (provisional) end of this story is very great. For Austin, the concept of the performative helps us to think about a particular aspect of language neglected by prior philosophers; for Butler, it is a model for thinking about crucial social processes where a number of matters are at stake: (1) the nature of identity and how it is produced; (2) the functioning of social norms; (3) the fundamental problem of what today we call "agency" in English: how far and under what conditions can I be a responsible subject who chooses my acts; and (4) the relationship between the individual and social change.

There is, thus, a big difference between what is at stake for Austin and for Butler. And they seem to have principally in view different sorts of acts. Austin is interested in how the repetition of a formula on a single occasion makes something happen (you made a promise). For Butler this is a special case of the massive and obligatory repetition that produces historical and social realities (you become a woman).

This difference, in fact, brings us back to the problem about the nature of the literary event, where there are also two ways of thinking of it as performative. We can say that the literary work accomplishes a singular, specific act. It creates that reality which is the work, and its sentences accomplish something in particular in that work. For each work, one can try to specify what it and its parts accomplish, just as one can try to spell out what is promised in a particular act of promising. This, one might say, is the Austinian version of the literary event.

But on the other hand, we could also say that a work succeeds, becomes an event, by a massive repetition that takes up norms and, possibly, changes things. If a novel happens, it does so because, in its singularity, it inspires a passion that gives life to these forms, in acts of reading and recollection, repeating its inflection of the conventions of the novel and, perhaps, effecting an alteration in the norms or the forms through which readers go on to confront the world. A poem may very well disappear without a trace, but it may also trace itself in memories and give rise to acts of repetition. Its performativity isn't a singular act accomplished once and for all but a repetition that gives life to forms it repeats.

The concept of the performative, in the history I have outlined, brings together a series of issues that are crucial to "theory." Let me just list them:

First, how to think about the shaping role of language: do we try to limit it to certain specific acts, where we think we can say with confidence what it does, or do we try to gauge the broader effects of language, as it organizes our encounters with the world?

Second, how should we conceive of the relation between social conventions and individual acts? It is tempting, but too simple, to imagine that social conventions are like the scenery or background against which we decide how to act. Theories of the performative offer better accounts of the entanglement of norm and action, whether presenting conventions as the condition of possibility of events, as in Austin, or else, as in Butler, seeing action as obligatory repetition, which may nevertheless deviate from the norms. Literature, which is supposed to "make it new" in a space of convention, calls for a performative account of norm and event.

Third, how should one conceive of the relation between what language does and what it says? This is the basic problem of the performative: can there be a harmonious fusion of doing and saying or is there an unavoidable tension here that governs and complicates all textual activity?

Finally, how, in this postmodern age, should we think of the event? It has become commonplace in the United States, for instance, in this age of mass media, to say that what happens on television "happens period," is a real event. Whether the image corresponds to a reality or not, the mediatic event is a genuine event to be reckoned with. The model of the performative offers a more sophisticated account of issues that are often crudely stated as a blurring of the boundaries between fact and fiction. And the problem of literary event, of literature as act, can offer a model for thinking about cultural events generally.

EIGHT

Identity, Identification, and the Subject

●

The Subject

A LOT OF RECENT THEORETICAL DEBATE concerns the identity and function of the subject or self. What is this "I" that I am—person, agent or actor, self—and what makes it what it is? Two basic questions underlie modern thinking on this topic: first, is the self something given or something made and, second, should it be conceived in individual or in social

One of the challenges Odysseus faced in his ten-year journey home to Ithaca after the end of the Trojan War, chronicled in Homer's epic *The Odyssey*, was his encounter with the goddess Circe, who turned his scouting party into swine by giving them a magic potion. In *Circe Offering the Cup to Odysseus*, an 1891 oil on canvas by Pre-Raphaelite painter John William Waterhouse, Circe attempts to turn Odysseus into a swine as well, but, inoculated against her potion by the mythical herb moly, given to him by the god Hermes, he is able to withstand her magic and force her to change his sailors back into men. Odysseus is principally defined through his repeated struggles to save himself (successfully) and his sailors (unsuccessfully) and return home to Ithaca.

terms? These two oppositions generate four basic strands of modern thought. The first, opting for the given and the individual, treats the self, the "I," as something inner and unique, something that is prior to the acts it performs, an inner core which is variously expressed (or not expressed) in word and deed. The second, combining the given and the social, emphasizes that the self is determined by its origins and social attributes: you are male or female, white or black, British or American, and so on, and these are primary facts, givens of the subject or the self. The third, combining the individual and the made, emphasizes the changing nature of a self, which becomes what it is through its particular acts. Finally, the combination of the social and the made stresses that I become what I am through the various subject positions I occupy, as a boss rather than a worker, rich rather than poor.

The dominant modern tradition in the study of literature has treated the individuality of the individual as something given, a core which is expressed in word and deed and which can therefore be used to explain action: I did what I did because of who I am, and to explain what I did or said you should look back at the "I" (whether conscious or unconscious) that my words and acts express. "Theory" has contested not just this model of expression, where acts or words work by expressing a prior subject, but also the priority of the subject itself. Michel Foucault writes, "The researches of psychoanalysis, of linguistics, of anthropology have 'decentered' the subject in relation to the laws of its desire, the forms of its language, the rules of its actions, or the play of its mythical and imaginative discourse." If the possibilities of thought and action are determined by a series of systems which the subject does not control or even understand, then the subject is "decentered" in the sense that it is not a source or center to which one refers to explain events. It is something formed by these forces. Thus, psychoanalysis treats the subject not as a unique essence but as the product of intersecting psychic, sexual, and linguistic mechanisms. Marxist theory sees the subject as determined by class position: it either profits from others' labor or labors for others' profit. Feminist theory stresses the impact of socially constructed gender roles on making the subject what he or she is. Queer theory has argued that the heterosexual subject is constructed through the repression of the possibility of homosexuality.

The question of the subject is "What am 'I'?" Am I made what I am by circumstances? What is the relation between the individuality of the individual and my identity as member of a group? And to what extent is the "I" that I am, the "subject," an agent who makes choices rather than has choices imposed on him or her? The English word *subject* already encapsulates this key theoretical problem: the subject is an actor or agent, a free subjectivity that does things, as in the "subject of a sentence." But a subject is also *subjected*, determined, "her Majesty the Queen's loyal subject," or the "subject of an experiment." Theory is inclined to argue that to be a subject at all is to be subjected to various regimes (psychosocial, sexual, linguistic).

Literature and Identity

Literature has always been concerned with questions about identity, and literary works sketch answers, implicitly or explicitly, to these questions. Narrative literature especially has followed the fortunes of characters as they define themselves and are defined by various combinations of their past, the choices they make, and the social forces that act upon them. Do characters *make* their fate or *suffer* it? Stories give different and complex answers. In the *Odyssey*, Odysseus is labelled "multiform" (*polytropos*) but defines himself in his struggles to save himself and his shipmates and to get home to Ithaca again. In Flaubert's *Madame Bovary*, Emma strives to define herself (or to "find herself") in relation to her romantic readings and her banal surroundings.

Literary works offer a range of implicit models of how identity is formed. There are narratives where identity is essentially determined by birth: the son of a king raised by shepherds is still fundamentally a king and rightfully becomes king when his identity is discovered. In other narratives characters change according to the changes in their fortunes, or else identity is based on personal qualities that are revealed during the tribulations of a life.

Nineteenth-century writer Gustave Flaubert, who was known for slaving over his manuscripts in search of *le mot juste,* took five years to complete his first novel, *Madame Bovary.* This work, for which Flaubert is most well-known, explores the role of fiction in distorting or making sense of experience: both the romantic novels Emma Bovary reads as well as Flaubert's own acerbic novel make sense of experience. This Alfred de Richemont composition, engraved by Charles Chessa, from the 1905 Librairie des Amateurs edition of Flaubert's *Madame Bovary,* shows Emma Bovary walking with Léon.

The explosion of recent theorizing about race, gender, and sexuality in the field of literary studies owes much to the fact that literature provides rich materials for complicating political and sociological accounts of the role of such factors in the construction of identity. Consider the question of whether the identity of the subject is something given or something constructed. Not only are both options amply represented in literature, but the complications or entanglements are frequently laid out for us, as in the common plot where characters, as we say, "discover" who they are, not by learning something about their past (say, about their birth) but by acting in such a way that they *become* what then turns out, in some sense, to have been their "nature."

This structure, where you have to *become* what you supposedly already were (as Aretha Franklin comes to feel like a natural woman), has emerged as a paradox or aporia for recent theory, but it has been at work all along in narratives. Western novels reinforce the notion of an essential self by suggesting that the self which emerges from trying encounters with the world was in some sense there all along, as the basis for the actions which, from the perspective of readers, bring this self into being. The fundamental identity of characters emerges as the result of actions, of struggles with the world, but then this identity is posited as the basis, even the cause of those actions.

A good deal of recent theory can be seen as an attempt to sort out the paradoxes that often inform the treatment of identity in literature. Literary works characteristically represent individuals, so struggles about identity are struggles within the individual and between individual and group: characters struggle against or comply with social norms and expectations. In theoretical writings, arguments about social identity tend to focus, though, on group identities: what is it to be a woman? to be black? Thus there are tensions between literary explorations and critical or theoretical claims. The power of literary representations depends, I suggested in Chapter 2, on their special combination of singularity and exemplarity: readers encounter concrete portrayals of Prince Hamlet or Jane Eyre or Huckleberry Finn, and with them the presumption that these characters' problems are exemplary. But exemplary of what? The novels don't tell. It's the critics or theorists who have to take up the question of exemplarity and tell us what group or class of people the character stands for: is Hamlet's condition "universal"? Is Jane Eyre's the predicament of women in general?

Theoretical treatments of identity may seem reductive in comparison with the subtle explorations in novels, which are able to finesse the problem of general claims by presenting singular cases while relying on a generalizing force that is left implicit—perhaps we are all Oedipus, or Hamlet, or Madame Bovary, or Janie Starks. When novels are concerned with group identities—what it is to be a woman, or child of the bourgeoisie—they frequently explore how the demands of group identity restrict individual possibilities. Theorists have therefore argued that novels, by making the individuality of the individual their central focus, construct an ideology of individual identity whose neglect of larger social issues critics should question. Emma Bovary's problem, you can argue, is not her foolishness or her infatuation with romances but the general situation of women in her society.

Literature has not only made identity a theme; it has played a significant role in the construction of the identity of readers. The value of literature has long been linked to the vicarious experiences it gives readers, enabling them to know how it feels to be in particular situations and thus to acquire dispositions to act and feel in certain ways. Literary works encourage identification with characters by showing things from their point of view.

Poems and novels address us in ways that demand identification, and identification works to create identity: we become who we are by identifying with figures we read about. Literature has long been blamed for encouraging the young to see themselves as characters in novels and to seek fulfillment in analogous ways: running away from home to experience the life of the metropolis, espousing the values of heroes and heroines in revolting against their elders and feeling disgust at the world before having experienced it, or making their lives a quest for love and trying to reproduce scenarios of novels and love lyrics. Literature is said to corrupt through mechanisms of identification. The champions of literary education have hoped, on the contrary, that literature would make us better people through vicarious experience and the mechanisms of identification.

Representing or Producing?

Does discourse represent identities that already exist or does it produce them? This has been a major theoretical issue. Foucault, as we saw in Chapter 1, treats "the homosexual" as an identity invented by discursive practices in the nineteenth century. The American critic Nancy Armstrong argues that eighteenth-century novels and conduct books—books about how to behave—produced "the modern individual," who was first of all a woman. The modern individual, in this sense, is a person whose identity and worth are thought to come from feelings and personal qualities rather than from his or her place in the social hierarchy. This is an identity gained through love and centered in the domestic sphere rather than in society. Such a notion has now gained wide currency—the true self is the one you find through love and through your relations with family and friends—but it begins in the eighteenth and nineteenth centuries as an idea about the

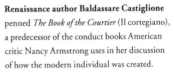

Renaissance author Baldassare Castiglione
penned *The Book of the Courtier* (Il cortegiano),
a predecessor of the conduct books American
critic Nancy Armstrong uses in her discussion
of how the modern individual was created.

identity of women and only later is extended to men. Armstrong claims
that this concept is developed and extended by novels and other discourses
that champion feelings and private virtues. Today this concept of identity
is sustained by films, television, and a wide range of discourses, whose
scenarios tell us what it is to be a person, a man or a woman.

Psychoanalysis

Recent theory has, in fact, fleshed out what was often implicit in discussions of literature in treating identity as formed by a process of identification. For Freud, identification is a psychological process in which the
subject assimilates an aspect of the other and is transformed, wholly or
partially, according to the model that the other provides. The personality
or the self is constituted by a series of identifications. Thus, the basis of
sexual identity is an identification with a parent: one desires as the parent

does, as if imitating the parent's desire and becoming a rival for the loved object. In the Oedipus complex the boy identifies with the father and desires the mother.

Later psychoanalytic theories of the formation of identity debate the best way of thinking about the mechanism of identification. Jacques Lacan's account of what he calls "the mirror stage" locates the beginnings of identity in the moment when the infant identifies with his or her image in the mirror, perceiving himself or herself as whole, as what he or she wants to be. The self is constituted by what is reflected back: by a mirror, by the mother, and by others in social relations generally. Identity is the product of a series of partial identifications, never completed. Ultimately,

The mirror stage was twentieth-century French psychiatrist and psychoanalyst Jacques Lacan's first important contribution to the field of psychoanalysis. He initially presented the concept in the 1930s but some years later reworked his concept, creating a more complex theory.

psychoanalysis reaffirms the lesson one might draw from the most serious and celebrated novels: that identity is a failure; that we do not happily become men or women, that the internalization of social norms (which sociologists theorize as something that happens smoothly and inexorably) always encounters resistance and ultimately does not work: we do not become who we are supposed to be.

Theorists have recently given a further twist to the fundamental role of identification. Mikkel Borch-Jakobsen argues that

> Desire (the desiring subject) does not come first, to be *followed* by an identification that would allow the desire to be fulfilled. What comes first is a tendency toward identification, a primordial tendency which then gives rise to a desire . . . ; identification brings the desirous subject into being, not the other way around.

In the earlier model, desire is the bottom line; here identification precedes desire, and the identification with another involves imitation or rivalry that is the source of desire. This accords with scenarios in novels where, as René Girard and Eve Sedgwick argue, desire arises from identification and rivalry: heterosexual male desire flows from the hero's identification with a rival and imitation of his desire.

Group Identities

Identification also plays a role in the production of group identities. For members of historically oppressed or marginalized groups, stories prompt identification with a potential group and work to make the group a group by showing them who or what they might be. Theoretical debate in this area has focused most intensely on the desirability and political usefulness of different conceptions of identity: must there be something essential members of a group share if they are to function as a group? Or are claims about what it is to be a woman or to be black or to be gay oppressive, restrictive, and objectionable? Often the debate has been cast as a quarrel about "essentialism": between a notion of identity as something given, an origin, and a notion of identity as something always in process, arising through contingent alliances and oppositions (an oppressed people gain identity from opposing the oppressor).

The main question may be, what is the relation between critiques of essentialist conceptions of identity (of a person or group) and the psychic and political demands for identity? How do the urgencies of emancipatory politics, which seeks solid identities for women, or blacks, or the Irish, for instance, engage or conflict with psychoanalytic notions of the unconscious and a divided subject? This becomes a major theoretical as well as practical issue because the problems encountered seem similar, whether the groups in question are defined by nationality, race, gender, sexual preference, language, class, or religion. For historically marginalized groups, there are two processes under way: on the one hand, critical investigations demonstrate the illegitimacy of taking certain traits, such as sexual orientation, gender, or visible morphological characteristics, as essentially defining features of group identity, and refute the imputation of essential identity to all members of a group characterized by gender, class, race, religion, sexuality, or nationality. On the other hand, groups may make identities imposed on them into resources for that group. Foucault notes in *The History of Sexuality* that the emergence, in the nineteenth century, of medical and psychiatric discourses defining homosexuals as a deviant class facilitated social control, but also made possible "the formation of a 'reverse' discourse: homosexuality began to speak in its own behalf, to demand that its legitimacy or 'naturality' be acknowledged, often in the same vocabulary, using the same categories by which it was medically disqualified."

Pervasive Structures

What makes the problem of identity crucial and unavoidable are the tensions and conflicts it encapsulates (in this it resembles "meaning"). Work in theory emanating from different directions—Marxism, psychoanalysis, cultural studies, feminism, gay and lesbian studies, and the study of identity in colonial and post-colonial societies—has revealed difficulties involving identity that seem structurally similar. Whether, with Louis Althusser, we say that one is "culturally interpellated" or hailed as a subject, made a subject by being addressed as the occupant of a certain position or role; or whether we stress, with psychoanalysis, the role of a "mirror stage" in which the subject acquires identity by misrecognizing him- or herself in an image; whether, with Stuart Hall, we define identities as "the names we give to the different ways we are positioned by, and position ourselves in, the narratives of the past"; or whether we stress, as in studies of colonial and post-colonial subjectivity, the construction of a divided subject through the clash of contradictory discourses and demands; or whether, with Judith Butler, we see heterosexual identity as based on the repression of the possibility of homoerotic desire, we find something like a common mechanism. The process of identity formation not only foregrounds some differences and neglects others; it takes an internal difference or division and projects it as a difference between individuals or groups. To "be a man," as we say, is to deny any "effeminacy" or weakness and to project it as a difference *between* men and women. A difference *within* is denied and projected as a difference *between*. Work in a range of fields seems to be converging in its investigation of the ways in which subjects are produced by unwarranted if inevitable positings of unity and identity, which may be strategically empowering but also create gaps between the identity or role attributed to individuals and the varied events and positionings of their lives.

One source of confusion has been an assumption which often structures debate in this area, that internal divisions in the subject somehow foreclose the possibility of agency, of responsible action. A simple answer might be that those who demand more stress on agency want theories to say that deliberate actions will change the world and are frustrated by the fact that this may not be true. Do we not live in a world where acts are more likely to have unintended than intended consequences? But there are two more complex answers. First, as Judith Butler explains, "the reconceptualization of identity as an *effect*, that is, as *produced* or *generated* opens up possibilities of 'agency' that are insidiously foreclosed by positions that take identity categories as foundational and fixed." Speaking of gender as a compulsory performance, Butler locates agency in the variations of action, the possibilities of variation in repetition that carry meaning and create identity. Second, traditional conceptions of the subject in fact work to limit responsibility and agency. If the subject means "the conscious subject," then you can claim innocence, deny responsibility, if you haven't consciously chosen or intended the consequences of an act you have committed. If, on the contrary, your conception of the subject includes the unconscious and the subject positions you occupy, responsibility can be expanded. Emphasis on the structures of the unconscious or subject positions you do not choose calls you to responsibility for events and structures in your life—of racism and sexism, for instance—that you did not explicitly intend. The expanded notion of the subject combats the restriction of agency and responsibility derived from traditional conceptions of the subject.

Does the "I" freely choose or is it determined in its choices? The philosopher Anthony Appiah notes that this debate about agency and subject position involves two different levels of theory which are not really in competition, except that we can't engage in both at the same time. Talk about agency and choice flows from our concern to live intelligible lives among other people, to whom we ascribe beliefs and intentions. Talk about subject positions that determine action comes from our interest in understanding social and historical processes, in which individuals figure as socially determined. Some of the fiercest conflicts in contemporary theory arise when claims about individuals as agents and claims about the power of social and discursive structures are seen as competing causal explanations. In studies of identity in colonial and post-colonial societies, for instance, there has been heated debate about the agency of the native or "subaltern" (the term for a subordinate or inferior). Some thinkers, interested in the point of view and agency of the subaltern, have stressed acts of resistance to or compliance with colonialism, and are then accused of ignoring the most insidious effect of colonialism: the way it defined the situation and the possibilities of action, making the inhabitants "natives," for example. Other theorists, describing the pervasive power of "colonial discourse," the discourse of colonial powers which creates the world in which colonized subjects live and act, are accused of denying agency to the native subject.

According to Appiah's argument, these different sorts of accounts are not in conflict: the natives are still agents, and a language of agency is still appropriate, no matter how much the possibilities of action are defined by colonialist discourse. The two accounts belong to different registers, just as do an account of the decisions that led John to buy a new Mazda, on the one hand, and a description of the workings of global capitalism and the marketing of Japanese cars in America, on the other. There is much to be gained, Appiah claims, from separating the concepts of subject position and of agency, recognizing that they belong to different sorts of narratives. The energy from these theoretical disputes could then be redirected to questions about how identities are constructed and what role discursive practices, such as literature, play in these constructions.

But the possibility that accounts of subjects who choose and accounts of forces that determine subjects might peacefully coexist, as different narratives, seems remote. What drives theory, after all, is the desire to see how far an idea or argument can go and to question alternative accounts and their presuppositions. To pursue the idea of the agency of subjects is to take it as far as one can, to seek out and challenge positions that limit or counter it.

Theory

There may be a general lesson here. Theory, we might conclude, does not give rise to harmonious solutions. It doesn't, for instance, teach us, once and for all, what meaning is: how much the factors of intention, text, reader, and context each contribute to a sum that is meaning. Theory doesn't tell us whether poetry is a transcendent vocation or rhetorical trick or how much of each. Repeatedly I have found myself ending a chapter by invoking a tension between factors or perspectives or lines of argument and concluding that you have to pursue each, shifting between alternatives that cannot be avoided but that give rise to no synthesis. Theory, then, offers not a set of solutions but the prospect of further thought. It calls for commitment to the work of reading, of challenging presuppositions, of questioning the assumptions on which you proceed. I began by saying that theory was endless—an unbounded corpus of challenging and fascinating writings— but not just more writings: it is also an ongoing project of thinking which does not end when an introduction ends.

APPENDIX: THEORETICAL
SCHOOLS AND MOVEMENTS

•

I have chosen to introduce theory by presenting issues and debates rather than "schools," but readers have a right to expect an explanation of terms like *structuralism* and *deconstruction* that appear in discussions of criticism. I provide that here, in a brief description of modern theoretical movements.

Literary theory is not a disembodied set of ideas but a force in institutions. Theory exists in communities of readers and writers, as a discursive practice, inextricably entangled with educational and cultural institutions. Three theoretical modes whose impact, since the 1960s, has been greatest are the wide-ranging reflection on language, representation, and the categories of critical thought undertaken by deconstruction and psychoanalysis (sometimes in concert, sometimes in opposition); the analyses of the role of gender and sexuality in every aspect of literature and criticism by feminism and then gender studies and queer theory; and the development of historically oriented cultural criticisms (new historicism, post-colonial theory) studying a wide range of discursive practices, involving many objects (the body, the family, race) not previously thought of as having a history.

There are several important theoretical movements prior to the 1960s.

RUSSIAN FORMALISM

The Russian Formalists of the early years of the twentieth century stressed that critics should concern themselves with the literariness of literature: the verbal strategies that make it literary, the foregrounding of language itself, and the "making strange" of experience that they accomplish. Redirecting attention from authors to verbal "devices," they claimed that "the device is the only hero of literature." Instead of asking "What does the author say here?" we should ask something like "What happens to the sonnet here?" or "What adventures befall the novel in this book by Dickens?" Roman Jakobson, Boris Eichenbaum, and Victor Shklovsky are three key figures in this group which reoriented literary study toward questions of form and technique.

NEW CRITICISM

What is called the "New Criticism" arose in the United States in the 1930s and 1940s (with related work in England by I. A. Richards and William Empson). It focused attention on the unity or integration of literary works. Opposed to the historical scholarship practiced in universities, the New Criticism treated poems as aesthetic objects rather than historical documents and examined the interactions of their verbal features and the ensuing complications of meaning rather than the historical intentions and circumstances of their authors. For new critics (Cleanth Brooks, John Crowe Ransom, W. K. Wimsatt), the task of criticism was to elucidate individual works of art. Focusing on ambiguity, paradox, irony, and the effects of connotation and poetic imagery, the New Criticism sought to show the contribution of each element of poetic form to a unified structure.

The New Criticism left as enduring legacies techniques of close reading and the assumption that the test of any critical activity is whether it helps us to produce richer, more insightful interpretations of individual works. But beginning in the 1960s, a number of theoretical perspectives and discourses—phenomenology, linguistics, psychoanalysis, Marxism, structuralism, feminism, deconstruction—offered richer conceptual frameworks than did the New Criticism for reflecting on literature and other cultural products.

PHENOMENOLOGY

Phenomenology emerges from the work of the early-twentieth-century philosopher Edmund Husserl. It seeks to bypass the problem of the separation between subject and object, consciousness and the world, by focusing on the phenomenal reality of objects as they appear to consciousness. We can suspend questions about the ultimate reality or knowability of the world and describe the world as it is given to consciousness. Phenomenology underwrote criticism devoted to describing the "world" of an author's consciousness, as manifested in the entire range of his or her works (Georges Poulet, J. Hillis Miller). But more important has been "reader-response criticism" (Stanley Fish, Wolfgang Iser). For the reader, the work is what is given to consciousness; one can argue that the work is not something objective, existing independently of any experience of it, but is the experience of the reader. Criticism can thus take the form of a description of the reader's progressive movement through a text, analyzing how readers produce meaning by making connections, filling in things left unsaid, anticipating and conjecturing and then having their expectations disappointed or confirmed.

Another reader-oriented version of phenomenology is called "aesthetics of reception" (Hans Robert Jauss). A work is an answer to questions posed by a "horizon of expectations." The interpretation of works should, therefore, focus not on the experience of an individual reader but on the history of a work's reception and its relation to the changing aesthetic norms and sets of expectations that allow it to be read in different eras.

STRUCTURALISM

Reader-oriented theory has something in common with structuralism, which also focuses on how meaning is produced. But structuralism originated in *opposition* to phenomenology: instead of describing experience, the goal was to identify the underlying structures that make it possible. In place of the phenomenological description of consciousness, structuralism sought to analyze structures that operate unconsciously (structures of language, of the psyche, of society). Because of its interest in how meaning is produced, structuralism often (as in Roland Barthes's *S/Z*) treated the reader as the site of underlying codes that make meaning possible and as the agent of meaning.

Structuralism usually designates a group of primarily French thinkers who, in the 1950s and 1960s, influenced by Ferdinand de Saussure's theory of language, applied concepts from structural linguistics to the study of social and cultural phenomena. Structuralism developed first in anthropology (Claude Lévi-Strauss), then in literary and cultural studies (Roman Jakobson, Roland Barthes, Gérard Genette), psychoanalysis (Jacques Lacan), intellectual history (Michel Foucault), and Marxist theory (Louis Althusser). Although these thinkers never formed a school as such, it was under the label "structuralism" that their work was imported and read in England, the United States, and elsewhere in the late 1960s and 1970s.

In literary studies structuralism promotes a poetics interested in the conventions that make literary works possible; it seeks not to produce new interpretations of works but to understand how they can have the meanings and effects that they do. But it did not succeed in imposing this project

—a systematic account of literary discourse—in Britain and America. Its main effect there was to offer new ideas about literature and to make it one signifying practice among others. It thus opened the way to symptomatic readings of literary works and encouraged cultural studies to try to spell out the signifying procedures of different cultural practices.

It is not easy to distinguish structuralism from *semiotics*, the general science of signs, which traces its lineage to Saussure and the American philosopher Charles Sanders Peirce. Semiotics, though, is an international movement that has sought to incorporate the scientific study of behavior and communication, while mostly avoiding the philosophical speculation and cultural critique that has marked structuralism in its French and related versions.

POST-STRUCTURALISM

Once structuralism came to be defined as a movement or school, theorists distanced themselves from it. It became clear that works by alleged structuralists did not fit the idea of structuralism as an attempt to master and codify structures. Barthes, Lacan, and Foucault, for example, were identified as *post-structuralists*, who had gone beyond structuralism narrowly conceived. But many positions associated with post-structuralism are evident even in the early work of these thinkers when they were seen as structuralists. They had described ways in which theories get entangled in the phenomena they attempt to describe; how texts create meaning by violating any conventions that structural analysis locates. They recognized the impossibility of describing a complete or coherent signifying system, since systems are always changing. In fact, post-structuralism does not demonstrate the inadequacies or errors of structuralism so much as turn away from the project of working out what makes cultural phenomena intelligible and emphasize instead a critique of knowledge, totality, and the subject. It treats each of these as a problematical effect. The structures of the systems of signification do not exist independently of the subject, as objects of knowledge, but are structures for subjects, who are entangled with the forces that produce them.

DECONSTRUCTION

The term *post-structuralism* is used for a broad range of theoretical discourses in which there is a critique of notions of objective knowledge and of a subject able to know him- or herself. Thus, contemporary feminisms, psychoanalytic theories, Marxisms, and historicisms all partake in post-structuralism. But *post-structuralism* also designates above all *deconstruction* and the work of Jacques Derrida, who first came to prominence in America with a critique of the structuralist notion of structure in the very collection of essays that brought structuralism to American attention (*The Languages of Criticism and the Sciences of Man*, 1970).

Deconstruction is most simply defined as a critique of the hierarchical oppositions that have structured Western thought: inside/outside, mind/body, literal/metaphorical, speech/writing, presence/absence, nature/culture, form/meaning. To deconstruct an opposition is to show that it is not natural and inevitable but a construction, produced by discourses that rely on it, and to show that it is a construction in a work of *de*construction that seeks to dismantle it and reinscribe it—that is, not destroy it but give it a different structure and functioning. But as a mode of reading, deconstruction is, in Barbara Johnson's phrase, a "teasing out of warring forces of signification within a text," an investigation of the tension between modes of signification, as between the performative and constative dimensions of language.

In so far as feminism undertakes to deconstruct the opposition man/woman and the oppositions associated with it in the history of Western culture, it is a version of post-structuralism, but that is only one strand of feminism, which is less a unified school than a social and intellectual movement and a space of debate. On the one hand, feminist theorists champion the identity of women, demand rights for women, and promote women's writings as representations of the experience of women. On the other hand, feminists undertake a theoretical critique of the heterosexual matrix that organizes identities and cultures in terms of the opposition between man and woman. Elaine Showalter distinguishes "the feminist critique" of male assumptions and procedures from "gynocriticism," a feminist criticism concerned with women authors and the representation of women's experience. Both of these modes have been opposed to what is sometimes called, in Britain and America, "French feminism," where "woman" comes to stand for any radical force that subverts the concepts, assumptions, and structures of patriarchal discourse. Similarly, feminist theory includes both strands that reject psychoanalysis for its incontrovertibly sexist foundations and the brilliant rearticulation of psychoanalysis by such feminist scholars as Jacqueline Rose, Mary Jacobus, and Kaja Silverman, for whom it is only through psychoanalysis, with its understanding of the complications of internalizing norms, that one can hope to comprehend and reconceive the predicament of women. In its multiple projects, feminism has effected a substantial transformation of literary education in the United States and Britain, through its expansion of the literary canon and the introduction of a range of new issues.

PSYCHOANALYSIS

Psychoanalytic theory had an impact on literary studies both as a mode of interpretation and as a theory about language, identity, and the subject. On the one hand, along with Marxism it is the most powerful modern hermeneutic: an authoritative meta-language or technical vocabulary that can be applied to literary works, as to other situations, to understand what is "really" going on. This leads to a criticism alert to psychoanalytic themes and relations. But on the other hand, the greatest impact of psychoanalysis has come through the work of Jacques Lacan, a renegade French psychoanalyst who set up his own school outside the analytic establishment and led what he presented as a return to Freud. Lacan describes the subject as an effect of language and emphasizes the crucial role in analysis of what Freud called transference, in which the analysand casts the analyst in the role of authority figure from the past ("falling in love with your analyst"). The truth of the patient's condition, in this account, emerges not from the analyst's interpretation of the patient's discourse but from the way analyst and patient are caught up in replaying a crucial scenario from the patient's past. This reorientation makes psychoanalysis a post-structuralist discipline in which interpretation is a replaying of a text it does not master.

MARXISM

In Britain, unlike the United States, post-structuralism arrived not through Derrida and then Lacan and Foucault but through the work of the Marxist theorist Louis Althusser. Read within the Marxist culture of the British Left, Althusser led his readers to Lacanian theory and provoked a gradual transformation by which, as Antony Easthope puts it, "post-structuralism came to occupy much the same space as that of its host culture, Marxism." For Marxism, texts belong to a superstructure determined by the economic base (the "real relations of production"). To interpret cultural products is to relate them back to the base. Althusser argued that the social formation is not a unified totality with the mode of production at its center but a looser structure in which different levels or types of practice develop on different timescales. Social and ideological superstructures have a "relative autonomy." Drawing on a Lacanian account of the determination of consciousness by the unconscious for an explanation of how ideology functions to determine the subject, Althusser maps a Marxist account of the determination of the individual by the social onto psychoanalysis. The subject is an effect constituted in the processes of the unconscious, of discourse, and of the relatively autonomous practices that organize society.

This conjunction is the basis of much theoretical debate in Britain, in political theory as well as literary and cultural studies. Crucial investigations of relations between culture and signification took place in the 1970s in the film studies magazine *Screen*, which, deploying Althusser and Lacan, sought to understand how the subject is positioned or constructed by the structures of cinematic representation.

NEW HISTORICISM/CULTURAL MATERIALISM

The 1980s and 1990s in Britain and the United States were marked by the emergence of vigorous, theoretically engaged historical criticism. On the one hand, there is British *cultural materialism*, defined by Raymond Williams as "the analysis of all forms of signification, including quite centrally writing, within the actual means and conditions of their production." Renaissance specialists influenced by Foucault (Catherine Belsey, Jonathan Dollimore, Alan Sinfield, and Peter Stallybrass) have been particularly concerned with the historical constitution of the subject and with the contestatory role of literature in the Renaissance. In the United States, *new historicism*, which is less inclined to posit a hierarchy of cause and effect as it traces connections among texts, discourses, power, and the constitution of subjectivity, has also been centered on the Renaissance. Stephen Greenblatt, Louis Montrose, and others focus on how Renaissance literary texts are situated amid the discursive practices and the institutions of the period, treating literature not as a reflection or product of a social reality but as one of several sometimes antagonistic practices. A key question for the new historicists has been the dialectic of "subversion and containment": how far do Renaissance texts offer a genuinely radical critique of the religious and political ideologies of their day and how far is the discursive practice of literature, in its apparent subversiveness, a way of containing subversive energies?

POST-COLONIAL THEORY

A related set of theoretical questions emerge in *post-colonial* theory: the attempt to understand the problems posed by the European colonization and its aftermath. In this legacy, post-colonial institutions and experiences, from the idea of the independent nation to the idea of culture itself, are entangled with the discursive practices of the West. Since the 1980s a growing corpus of writings has debated questions about the relation between the hegemony of Western discourses and the possibilities of resistance, and about the formation of colonial and post-colonial subjects: hybrid subjects, emerging from the superimposition of conflicting languages and cultures. Edward Said's *Orientalism* (1978), which examined the construction of the oriental "other" by European discourses of knowledge, helped to establish the field. Since then post-colonial theory and writing have become an attempt to intervene in the construction of culture and knowledge, and, for intellectuals who come from post-colonial societies, to write their way back into a history others have written.

MINORITY DISCOURSE

One political change that has been achieved within academic institutions in the United States has been the growth of study of literatures of ethnic minorities. The main effort has been to revive and promote the study of black, Latino, Asian American, and Native American writing. Debates bear on the relation between the strengthening of cultural identity of particular groups by linking it to a tradition of writing and the liberal goal of celebrating cultural diversity and "multiculturalism." Theoretical questions swiftly become entangled with questions about the status of theory, which is sometimes said to impose "white" questions or philosophical issues on projects struggling to establish their own terms and contexts. But Latino, African American, and Asian American critics pursue the theoretical enterprise in developing the study of minority discourses, defining their distinctiveness, and articulating their relations to dominant traditions of writing and thought. Attempts to generate theories of "minority discourse" both develop concepts for the analysis of specific cultural traditions and use a position of marginality to expose the assumptions of "majority" discourse and to intervene in its theoretical debates.

QUEER THEORY

Like deconstruction and other contemporary theoretical movements, queer theory (discussed in Chapter 7) uses the marginal—what has been set aside as perverse, beyond the pale, radically other—to analyze the cultural construction of the center: heterosexual normativity. In the work of Eve Sedgwick, Judith Butler, and others, queer theory has become the site of a productive questioning not just of the cultural construction of sexuality but of culture itself, as based on the denial of homoerotic relations. As with feminism and versions of ethnic studies before it, it gains intellectual energy from its link with social movements of liberation and from the debates within these movements about appropriate strategies and concepts. Should one celebrate and accentuate difference or challenge distinctions that stigmatize? How to do both? Possibilities of both action and understanding are at stake in theory.

REFERENCES

•

CHAPTER 1

Richard Rorty, *Consequences of Pragmatism* (Minneapolis: University of Minnesota Press, 1982), 66. Michel Foucault, *The History of Sexuality*, vol. I (New York: Pantheon, 1980), 154, 156, 43. SPEECH AND WRITING: Jonathan Culler, *On Deconstruction: Theory and Criticism After Structuralism* (Ithaca, NY: Cornell University Press, 1982), 89–110. Jean-Jacques Rousseau, *Confessions*, Book 3, and elsewhere, quoted in Jacques Derrida, *Of Grammatology* (Baltimore: Johns Hopkins University Press, 1976), 141–64. "IL N'Y A PAS DE HORS-TEXTE": Derrida, *Of Grammatology*, 158. ARETHA FRANKLIN: Judith Butler, "Imitation and Gender Insubordination," in *Inside/Out: Lesbian Theories, Gay Theories*, ed. Diana Fuss (New York: Routledge, 1991), 27–28.

CHAPTER 2

HISTORICAL UNDERSTANDING: W. B. Gallie, *Philosophy and the Historical Understanding* (London: Chatto, 1964), 65–71. WEED: John M. Ellis, *The Theory of Literary Criticism: A Logical Analysis* (Berkeley and Los Angeles: University of California Press, 1974), 37–42. HYPER-PROTECTED COOPERATIVE PRINCIPLE: Mary Louise Pratt, *Toward a Speech*

Act Theory of Literary Discourse (Bloomington: Indiana University Press, 1977), 38–78. Roman Jakobson, "Linguistics and Poetics," *Language in Literature* (Cambridge, MA: Harvard University Press, 1987), 70. Immanuel Kant, *The Critique of Judgment*, part 1, section 15. INTERTEXTUALITY: see Roland Barthes, *S/Z* (New York: Farrar Strauss, 1984), 10–12, 20–22, and Harold Bloom, *Poetry and Repression* (New Haven: Yale University Press, 1976), 2–3. Benedict Anderson, *Imagined Communities: Reflections on the Origin and Spread of Nationalism* (London: Verso, 1983), 40. ARTICLE OF 1860: H. Richardson, "On the Use of English Classical Literature in the Work of Education," quoted in Chris Baldick, *The Social Mission of English Criticism, 1848–1932* (Oxford: Clarendon, 1987), 66. Terry Eagleton, *Literary Theory: An Introduction* (Oxford: Blackwell, 1983), 25. CULTURAL CAPITAL: John Guillory, *Cultural Capital: The Problem of Literary Canon Formation* (Chicago: University of Chicago Press, 1993).

CHAPTER 3

CULTURAL STUDIES: Richard Klein, *Cigarettes Are Sublime* (Durham, NC: Duke University Press, 1993), and *Eat Fat* (New York: Pantheon, 1996); Marjorie Garber, *ViceVersa: Bisexuality and the Eroticism of Everyday Life* (New York: Simon & Schuster, 1994); Mark Seltzer, *Serial Killers I, II, III* (New York: Routledge, 1997). Roland Barthes, *Mythologies* (London: Cape, 1972), 15–25. Louis Althusser, "Ideology and Ideological State Apparatuses (Notes Toward an Investigation)," *Lenin and Philosophy, and Other Essays* (London: New Left Books, 1971), 168. AMERICAN COLLECTION: Lawrence Grossberg, Cary Nelson, and Paula Treichler, eds., *Cultural Studies* (New York: Routledge, 1992), 2, 4. SOCIAL TOTALITY: Ernesto Laclau, *New Reflections on the Revolution of Our Time* (London:

Verso, 1990), 89–92. POLICE SERIALS: Antony Easthope, *Literary into Cultural Studies* (London: Routledge, 1991), 109.

CHAPTER 4

Ferdinand de Saussure, *Course in General Linguistics* (London: Duckworth, 1983), 107, 115. B. L. Whorf, *Language, Thought and Reality* (Cambridge, MA: MIT Press, 1956). LITERARY COMPETENCE: Jonathan Culler, *Structuralist Poetics: Structuralism, Linguistics, and the Study of Literature* (London: Routledge & Kegan Paul, 1975), 113–60. HORIZON OF EXPECTATIONS: Robert Holub, *Reception Theory: A Critical Introduction* (London: Methuen, 1984), 58–63. Elaine Showalter, "Towards a Feminist Poetics," in *Women Writing and Writing about Women*, ed. Mary Jacobus (London: Croom Helm, 1979), 25. INTENTIONAL FALLACY: W. K. Wimsatt and Monroe Beardsley, "The Intentional Fallacy," in Wimsatt, *The Verbal Icon: Studies in the Meaning of Poetry* (Lexington: University of Kentucky Press, 1954), 18. Toni Morrison, *Playing in the Dark: Whiteness and the American Literary Imagination* (Cambridge, MA: Harvard University Press, 1992). Edward Said, "Jane Austen and Empire," *Culture and Imperialism* (New York: Knopf, 1993), 80–97. HERMENEUTICS OF SUSPICION: Hans-Georg Gadamer, "The Hermeneutics of Suspicion," in *Hermeneutics: Questions and Prospects*, ed. Gary Shapiro and Alan Sica (Amherst: University of Massachusetts Press, 1984), 54–65.

CHAPTER 5

Jacques Derrida, "White Mythology: Metaphor in the Text of Philosophy," *Margins of Philosophy* (Chicago: University of Chicago Press, 1982), 207–71. RHETORICAL FIGURES: Jonathan Culler, "The Turns of Metaphor," *The Pursuit of Signs: Semiotics, Literature, Deconstruction* (London: Routledge &

Kegan Paul, 1981), 188–209. George Lakoff and Mark Johnson, *Metaphors We Live By* (Chicago: University of Chicago Press, 1980). Roman Jakobson, "Two Aspects of Language . . . ," *Language in Literature* (Cambridge, MA: Harvard University Press, 1987), 95–114. FOUR MASTER TROPES: Hayden White, *Tropics of Discourse: Essays in Cultural Criticism* (Baltimore: Johns Hopkins University Press, 1978), 5–6, 58–75. PRETENDS TO BE TALKING: Northrop Frye, *The Anatomy of Criticism: Four Essays* (Princeton, NJ: Princeton University Press, 1965), 249. FICTIONAL IMITATIONS: Barbara Herrnstein Smith, *On the Margins of Discourse: On the Relation of Language to Literature* (Chicago: University of Chicago Press, 1978), 30; Northrop Frye, *Anatomy of Criticism*, 271–72, 275, 280.

CHAPTER 6

Frank Kermode, *The Sense of an Ending* (Oxford: Oxford University Press, 1967), 45. Aristotle, *Poetics*, chapters 6–11. Mikhail Bakhtin, *The Dialogic Imagination: Four Essays* (Austin: University of Texas Press, 1981). Mieke Bal, *Narratology: Introduction to the Theory of Narrative*, 2nd ed. (Toronto: University of Toronto Press, 1997), 142–66. Gérard Genette, *Narrative Discourse: An Essay in Method* (Ithaca, NY: Cornell University Press, 1980), 189–211. PSEUDO-ITERATIVE: Genette, *Narrative Discourse*, 121–27. E. M. Forster, *Aspects of the Novel* (New York: Harcourt, 1927), 64. Paul de Man, *The Resistance to Theory* (Minneapolis: University of Minnesota Press, 1986), 11.

CHAPTER 7

J. L. Austin, *How to Do Things with Words* (Cambridge, MA: Harvard University Press, 1975), 5, 6, 14, 54–70, 9, 22. LITERARY CRITICS: Sandy Petrey, *Speech Acts and Literary Theory* (New York: Routledge, 1990).

Jacques Derrida, "Signature, Event, Context," *Margins of Philosophy* (Chicago: University of Chicago Press, 1983), 307–30. Jacques Derrida, *Acts of Literature*, ed. Derek Attridge (New York: Routledge, 1992), 55. DECLARATION OF INDEPENDENCE: Jacques Derrida, "Declarations of Independence," *New Political Science*, 15 (Summer 1986), 7–15. APORIA: Paul de Man, *Allegories of Reading* (New Haven: Yale University Press, 1979), 131. Judith Butler, *Gender Trouble: Feminism and the Subversion of Identity* (New York: Routledge, 1990), 136–41. Judith Butler, *Bodies That Matter: On the Discursive Limits of "Sex"* (New York: Routledge, 1993), 7, 2, 231–32, 226.

CHAPTER 8

Michel Foucault, *The Archeology of Knowledge* (New York: Pantheon, 1972), 22. QUEER THEORY: Judith Butler, *Bodies That Matter: On the Discursive Limits of "Sex"* (New York: Routledge, 1993), 235–40. Nancy Armstrong, *Desire and Domestic Fiction* (New York: Oxford University Press, 1987), 9. FREUD: Jean Laplanche and J. B. Pontalis, *The Language of PsychoAnalysis* (New York: Norton, 1973), 205–8. Jacques Lacan, "The Mirror Stage," *Écrits: A Selection* (New York: Norton, 1977), 1–7. Mikkel Borch-Jakobsen, *The Freudian Subject* (Stanford, CA: Stanford University Press, 1988), 47. René Girard, *Deceit, Desire and the Novel: Self and Other in Literary Structure* (Baltimore: Johns Hopkins University Press, 1965). Eve Kosofsky Sedgwick, *Between Men: English Literature and Male Homosocial Desire* (New York: Columbia University Press, 1985). URGENCIES OF EMANCIPATORY POLITICS: Jacqueline Rose, *Sexuality in the Field of Vision* (London: Verso, 1986), 103. Michel Foucault, *The History of Sexuality*, vol. I (New York: Random, 1978), 101. Stuart Hall, "Cultural Identity and Cinematic Representation," *Framework*, 36 (1987),

70. Difference Within: Barbara Johnson, "The Critical Difference: BartheS/BalZac," *The Critical Difference: Essays in the Contemporary Rhetoric of Reading* (Baltimore: Johns Hopkins University Press, 1980), 4. Judith Butler, *Gender Trouble: Feminism and the Subversion of Identity* (New York: Routledge, 1990), 147. Kwame Anthony Appiah, "Tolerable Falsehoods: Agency and the Interests of Theory," in *The Consequences of Theory*, ed. Jonathan Arac and Barbara Johnson (Baltimore: Johns Hopkins University Press, 1991), 74, 83. Subaltern: Gayatri Spivak, "Can the Subaltern Speak?" in Cary Nelson and Lawrence Grossberg, eds., *Marxism and the Interpretation of Culture* (Urbana: University of Illinois Press, 1988), 271–313.

APPENDIX

Jacques Derrida, "Structure, Sign, and Play in the Discourse of the Human Sciences," in *The Languages of Criticism and the Sciences of Man*, ed. R. Macksey and E. Donatos (Baltimore: Johns Hopkins University Press, 1970), 247–65. Barbara Johnson, *The Critical Difference* (Baltimore: Johns Hopkins University Press, 1980), 5. Elaine Showalter, "Towards a Feminist Poetics," in *Women Writing and Writing About Women*, ed. Mary Jacobus (London: Croom Helm, 1979), 25. Jacqueline Rose, *Sexuality in the Field of Vision* (London: Verso, 1986). Mary Jacobus, *Reading Woman: Essays in Feminist Criticism* (New York: Columbia University Press, 1986). Kaja Silverman, *Threshold of the Visible World* (New York: Routledge, 1996). Antony Easthope, *British Post-Structuralism Since 1968* (New York: Routledge, 1988), xiv. Raymond Williams, *Writing in Society* (London: Verso, 1984), 210.

FURTHER READING

•

CHAPTER 1

Jonathan Culler, *On Deconstruction: Theory and Criticism After Structuralism* (Ithaca, NY: Cornell University Press, 1982), begins with a discussion of theory in general. Richard Harland, *Superstructuralism: The Philosophy of Structuralism and Post-Structuralism* (London: Methuen, 1987), a broad and lively introductory survey. For Foucault, see Paul Rabinow, ed., *The Foucault Reader* (New York: Pantheon, 1984); Lois McNay, *Foucault: A Critical Introduction* (New York: Continuum, 1994). For Derrida, see Culler, *On Deconstruction*, 85–179; Geoffrey Bennington, *Jacques Derrida* (Chicago: University of Chicago Press, 1993).

CHAPTER 2

Paul Hernadi, ed., *What Is Literature?* (Bloomington: Indiana University Press, 1978), for a range of representative statements. Mary Louise Pratt, *Toward a Speech Act Theory of Literary Discourse* (Bloomington: Indiana University Press, 1977), argues against the notion of literature as a special kind of language. Barbara Herrnstein Smith, *On the Margins of Discourse: On the Relation of Language to Literature* (Chicago: University of Chicago Press, 1979), treats literary works as fictional imitations of "real" speech acts. Terry Eagleton, *Literary Theory: An Introduction* (Oxford: Blackwell, 1983), 1–53, on the idea of literature in general and literary studies in nineteenth-century Britain. Antony Easthope, *Literary into Cultural Studies* (London: Routledge, 1991), 1–61, a useful overview of traditional conceptions of literature. Jacques Derrida, "This Strange Institution Called Literature," in *Acts of Literature*, ed. Derek Attridge (New York: Routledge, 1992), 33–75.

CHAPTER 3

"Forum: Thirty-Two Letters on the Relation Between Cultural Studies and the Literary," *PMLA*, 112: 2 (March 1997), 257–86, a lively spectrum of current views. Antony Easthope, *Literary into Cultural Studies* (London: Routledge, 1991), surveys British developments. Tony Bennett et al., eds., *Culture, Ideology, and Social Process: A Reader* (London: Batsford & Open University Press, 1987), an anthology of classic British essays for the Open University's "Popular Culture" course. John Fiske, *Understanding Popular Culture* (Boston: Unwin, 1989), an accessible introduction. Simon During, ed., *The Cultural Studies Reader* (London: Routledge, 1993), and Mieke Bal, ed., *The Practice of Cultural Analysis* (Stanford, CA: Stanford University Press, 1999), two recent collections. Ioan Davies, *Cultural Studies and Beyond: Fragments of Empire* (London: Routledge, 1995), a shrewd recent history. LITERARY CANON: Robert von Hallberg, ed., *Canons* (Chicago: University of Chicago Press, 1984).

CHAPTER 4

Jonathan Culler, *Saussure* (London: Fontana, 1976; rev. ed., Ithaca, NY: Cornell University Press, 1986), an introduction to his thought and influence. M. A. K. Halliday, *Explorations in the Functions of Language* (London:

Arnold, 1973), essays relevant to literary studies. Roger Fowler, *Linguistic Criticism* (Oxford: Oxford University Press, 1996), a valuable introduction to language and the linguistic dimensions of literature. William Ray, *Literary Meaning: From Phenomenology to Deconstruction* (Oxford: Blackwell, 1984), develops a convincing narrative about different critical schools' approaches to meaning in literature. Nigel Fabb et al., eds., *The Linguistics of Writing: Arguments Between Language and Literature* (New York: Methuen, 1987), strong recent essays. POETICS: Jonathan Culler, *Structuralist Poetics* (London: Routledge, 1975); Roland Barthes, *S/Z* (New York: Hill & Wang, 1974), analysis of a Balzac story that switches between poetics and hermeneutics. HERMENEUTICS: Donald Marshall, "Literary Interpretation," in *Introduction to Scholarship in Modern Languages and Literatures*, ed. Joseph Gibaldi, 2nd ed. (New York: MLA, 1992), 159–82. READER-RESPONSE CRITICISM: Jane Tompkins, ed., *Reader-Response Criticism: From Formalism to Post-Structuralism* (Baltimore: Johns Hopkins University Press, 1980).

CHAPTER 5

RHETORIC: Renato Barilli, *Rhetoric* (Minneapolis: University of Minnesota Press, 1989), a historical survey of key issues. GENRES: Paul Hernadi, *Beyond Genre: New Directions in Literary Classification* (Ithaca, NY: Cornell University Press, 1972). APOSTROPHE: Jonathan Culler, "Apostrophe," *The Pursuit of Signs, Semiotics Literature, Deconstruction* (London: Routledge, 1981), 135–54. POETICS: Jonathan Culler, "Poetics of the Lyric," *Structuralist Poetics: Structuralism, Linguistics, and the Study of Literature* (London: Routledge & Kegan Paul, 1975), 161–88. POETRY: For a range of essays engaged with theoretical questions, Chaviva Hosek and Patricia Parker, eds., *Lyric Poetry: Beyond New*

Criticism (Ithaca, NY: Cornell University Press, 1985); Jacques Derrida, "What Is Poetry?" ("Che cos'è la poesia?"), in *A Derrida Reader: Between the Blinds*, ed. Peggy Kamuf (New York: Columbia University Press, 1991), 221–46.

CHAPTER 6

Two excellent, systematic books are Susan Lanser, *The Narrative Act: Point of View in Fiction* (Princeton, NJ: Princeton University Press, 1981), and Mieke Bal, *Narratology: Introduction to the Theory of Narrative*, 2nd rev. ed. (Toronto: University of Toronto Press, 1997). See also Wallace Martin, *Recent Theories of Narrative* (Ithaca, NY: Cornell University Press, 1986); Shlomith Rimmon-Kenan, *Narrative Fiction: Contemporary Poetics* (London: Methuen, 1983); Jonathan Culler, "Story and Discourse in the Analysis of Narrative," *The Pursuit of Signs: Semiotics, Literature, Deconstruction* (London: Routledge & Kegan Paul, 1981), 169–87; Jonathan Culler, "Poetics of the Novel," *Structuralist Poetics: Structuralism, Linguistics, and the Study of Literature* (London: Routledge & Kegan Paul, 1975), 189–238. DESIRE: Peter Brooks, *Psychoanalysis and Storytelling* (Oxford: Blackwell, 1994); Teresa de Lauretis, "Desire in Narrative," *Alice Doesn't* (Bloomington: Indiana University Press, 1984), 103–57. POLICING: D. A. Miller, *The Novel and the Police* (Berkeley and Los Angeles: University of California Press, 1988).

CHAPTER 7

Jacques Derrida, *Limited Inc.* (Evanston, IL: Northwestern University Press, 1988), includes "Signature, Event, Context" and other discussions of the performative. Barbara Johnson, "Poetry and Performative Language," *The Critical Difference: Essays in the Contemporary Rhetoric of Reading* (Baltimore: Johns Hopkins University Press, 1980), a short, efficient discussion. Shoshana Felman, *The Literary Speech Act* (Ithaca, NY: Cornell University Press, 1983), on Austin and Lacan.

CHAPTER 8

Charles Taylor, *Sources of the Self: The Making of the Modern Identity* (Cambridge, MA: Harvard University Press, 1989), a broad survey. Kaja Silverman, *The Subject of Semiotics* (Oxford: Oxford University Press, 1983), synthesizes psychoanalysis and semiotics on subject formation, with literary and cinematic examples. For essentialism: Diana Fuss, *Identification Papers* (New York: Routledge, 1995). For postcolonial theory: Homi Bhabha, *The Location of Culture* (New York: Routledge, 1994), and Ania Loomba, *Colonialism/Postcolonialism* (New York: Routledge, 1998).

APPENDIX

For the institutional history of criticism, Jonathan Culler, "Literary Criticism and the American University," in *Framing the Sign: Criticism and Its Institutions* (Oxford: Blackwell, 1988), 3–40; Gerald Graff, *Professing Literature: An Institutional History* (Chicago: University of Chicago Press, 1987); Chris Baldick, *Criticism and Literary Theory, 1890 to the Present* (London: Longman, 1996).

On schools, see Terry Eagleton's *Literary Theory: An Introduction* (Oxford: Blackwell, 1983), a tendentious but very lively account of all the "schools" except the Marxist criticism he embraces; Antony Easthope's *British Post-Structuralism Since 1968* (New York: Routledge, 1988), a sophisticated account of the fortunes of "theory" in Britain; Peter Barry's *Beginning Theory: An Introduction to Literary and Cultural Theory* (Manchester: Manchester University Press, 1995), a useful "school"-oriented textbook; and Raman Selden, ed., *The Cambridge History of Literary Criticism*, vol. VIII, *From Formalism to Poststructuralism* (Cambridge: Cambridge University Press, 1995), which covers major movements. Richard Harland's *Superstructuralism: The Philosophy of Structuralism and Post-Structuralism* (London: Methuen, 1987) is a broad and lively introductory survey; Keith Green and Jill LeBihan, *Critical Theory and Practice: A Coursebook* (London: Routledge, 1996), cleverly fuses the survey by school with approach by "topic."

INDEX

•

Page numbers in *italics* include illustrations and photographs/captions.

PICTURE CREDITS

•

COURTESY OF WIKIMEDIA COMMONS: ii: Erithraiesche Sibylle by Michelangelo and assistants for the Sistine Chapel, 1508–12; 4: Goethe memorial in Liepzig/Upload by Langer Thomas; 13: portrait of Jean-Jacques Rousseau, 1766/Yorck Project: 10.000 Meisterwerke der Malerei; 22: Franz Ferdinand and Sophie, Duchess of Hohenberg; 25b: Freud's sofa, Freud Museum, London/Upload by Konstantin Binder from http://www.londonleben.co.uk/london_leben/2004/12/das_sofa.html; 27bl: Shakespeare's *Hamlet*, second quarto; 29: detail of landscape with scenes from Virgil's *Aeneid* (1603), by Frederick van Valckenborch, Museum Boijmans Van Beuningen, Rotterdam; 30: Madame de Staël, from Evert A. Duyckinick, *Portrait Gallery of Eminent Men and Women in Europe and America*, New York, Johnson, Wilson, 1873/Upload from University of Texas Libraries; 39: Eisenhower presidential campaign, September 1952/Upload by Minesweeper at en.wikipedia from http://www.eisenhower.archives.gov/All_About_Ike/Presidential/1952Campaign/1952_Campaign.html; 56: *Milton Dictating Paradise Lost to His Daughters*/Yorck Project: 10.000 Meisterwerke der Malerei; 67: 3-11 Sir Philip Sidney, frontispiece from Sidney Lee, *Great Englishmen of the Sixteenth Century*, New York, Charles Scribner's Sons, 1904/Upload from http://www.marcdatabase.com/~lemur/lemur.com/garret/portraits/; 81: Gustave Courbet, portrait of Paul Verlaine, Galerie Chichio Haller, Zurich/Upload from www.bildindex.de, obj 00076302; 88: Ferdinand Victor Delacroix, *Hamlet and Horatio in the Graveyard*/Yorck Project: 10.000 Meisterwerke der Malerei; 94: *Plato and Aristotle*, or *Philosophy*, by Luca della Robbia, Museo dell'Opera del Duomo, Florence, Italy/Upload by Jastrow; 100: *Sappho*, by Gustav Klimt/Yorck Project: 10.000 Meisterwerke der Malerei; 103: *Robert Burns*, etching portrait (1896) by William Hole R. S. A., from *The Poetry of Burns*, centenary edition; 134: James Joyce, photo by C. Ruf, Zurich, ca. 1918/Upload from Cornell Joyce Collection, http://rmc.library.cornell.edu/joyce/writingchaos/index.html; 148: *Circe Offering the Cup to Odysseus* (1891), by John William Waterhouse, Oldham Art Gallery, Oxford, UK/Upload from http://en.wikipedia.org/wiki/Image:Circe_Offering_the_Cup_to_Odysseus.jpg; 152: illustration from Gustave Flaubert, *Madame Bovary*, Paris, Librairie des Amateurs, 1905, composition by Alfred de Richemont, engraved by Charles Chessa